"Convinced that we are made to see the face of God, Bruce and Carolyn Hindmarsh invite us to join them for a prayer retreat. What a privilege it is, as we take the place of Mary of Bethany, looking up in contemplation at our Lord. This immensely practical book centers on Jesus, encouraging us to use our memory and imagination, so that in him we may enter more deeply into the presence of God. The mature result of many years of spiritual guidance, *At the Feet of Jesus* is a sure guide for making your own personal or group retreat."
Hans Boersma, professor at Nashotah House Theological Seminary in Wisconsin and author of *Pierced by Love*

"Can we meet Jesus in real time—a personal encounter that is no less real than that which the first disciples had with Jesus? Are we merely talking about Jesus and reading about how the first disciples knew Jesus and heard his voice and dwelt in his love? Or can we, in like fashion, know Jesus and the grace of his immediate presence in our lives, no less so than those disciples? Here is the guide to precisely that: an experience of prayer that is no less immediate than that of Mary of Bethany."
Gordon T. Smith, executive director of Christian Higher Education Canada and author of *Your Calling Here and Now*

"In these beautifully crafted reflections on Mary's experiences of sitting at the feet of Jesus, Bruce and Carolyn Hindmarsh invite us to indwell both Mary's Bethany home and our own home. They bring to this invitation their own rich experiences of exploring this material with others in retreat settings as well as their own thoughtful biblical and theological attention to the narrative details of the relevant Gospel texts. As we respond to their invitation to enter imaginatively into these Gospel stories, we can anticipate the living Christ encountering us where we happen to live and work."
Trevor Hudson, author of *Seeking God* and *In Search of God's Will*

"*At the Feet of Jesus* is a book that Bruce and Carolyn Hindmarsh are uniquely qualified to write. It is informed by both their academic and experiential experience, and it is inspired by insights from devotion masters through the centuries, with a particular tip of the cap to Ignatius of Loyola. I think this is a book that would have made Dallas Willard smile—and perhaps is making him smile. This multiuse guide is written to help the reader increase awareness of the availability of friendship that is being offered by the very present and very loving Jesus. Pull up a second chair as you read."
Gary W. Moon, founding executive director of the Martin Institute and Dallas Willard Center at Westmont College and author of *Becoming Dallas Willard*

"*At the Feet of Jesus* is an invitation. The Hindmarshes welcome us to come in, remove our shoes, and take a spot on the floor next to them—and Mary of Bethany. In a series of meditations that are as beautiful as they are thoughtful, as theologically profound as they are deeply moving, Bruce and Carolyn invite us to sit at our Lord's feet. As you pray through this book, you'll encounter the love of Christ in an intimate and transformative way."
Paul J. Gutacker, executive director of Brazos Fellows

"*At the Feet of Jesus* offers a short and easy-to-use retreat guide sensitively blending the authors' experience of Jesuit methods of meditation with Benedictine lectio divina. The heart of the book comprises three meditations on the stories of Mary, Martha, and Lazarus, which help readers explore—in terms of faith, hope, and love—the spiritual dimensions of their lives. A final reflection, adapting the examen to these meditations, will help make the move from prayer back to life."
David Foster, professor of philosophy, Greek, and Latin at the Collegio Sant'Anselmo and author of *Reading with God*

"I've read lots of books on reading the Bible meditatively. Plain and simple, *At the Feet of Jesus* might be the best. Bruce and Carolyn Hindmarsh have gifted us with a wise, insightful, sensitive, and thorough little book that elicits our smiles, tears, deep joy, and willingness to change. They gently lead us into the mind and heart of Jesus. Buy it, read it slowly, follow the steps provided, and *At the Feet of Jesus* will lead you—without exaggeration—to the feet of Jesus. Very highly recommended."

Chris Hall, former president of Renovaré and author of *A Different Way*

"Combining and integrating the rich spiritual treasures of Ignatian and Puritan spirituality, Bruce and Carolyn Hindmarsh have crafted a welcome guide to reading some of the most popular Gospel stories of Christ. This book promises not only to assist readers to engage Scripture deeply but, more importantly, to experience Jesus in new and fresh ways. Readers who prayerfully follow their guidelines will find themselves both befriended and cherished as the beloved of Christ. This is a resource to savor and return to again and again."

Tom Schwanda, associate professor of Christian formation and ministry, emeritus, Wheaton College

"With this gem of an offering, Bruce and Carolyn Hindmarsh lead us into an intimate retreat experience at the feet of Jesus. Thoroughly grounded in biblical and theological understanding, and in both the formational wisdom of the early church and later Catholic as well as Protestant historical streams, they lead us into an abiding in the Scriptures as, with Mary of Bethany, we meet with our Lord Jesus. 'Study and prayer belong together,' they invite, and as we move through their rich material, we find our study becoming prayer and our reading becoming a loving encounter with Jesus."

Susan Currie, director of the Selah Certificate Program in Spiritual Direction at Leadership Transformations

"*At the Feet of Jesus* is balm for the longing soul. Bruce and Carolyn Hindmarsh, seasoned seminary professors and spiritual guides, bring Scripture alive in its context, history, and sensory embodiment, allowing each reader to encounter Jesus in his fullness even in the midst of our own particular lives. With this guided retreat we accompany Mary of Bethany as she attends to Jesus with faith, hope, and love. One can almost see the meal in Martha's kitchen, feel the roughness of Lazarus's tomb, and smell the nard Mary lovingly pours on the Lord's feet. The fragrance of the holy fills us . . . and lingers."

Susan S. Phillips, sociologist, spiritual director, and author of *Candlelight: Illuminating the Art of Spiritual Direction*

"*At the Feet of Jesus* is a thoughtful, accessible, and deeply challenging collection of devotional meditations from Scripture that take us through the character of Mary of Bethany. Mary's posture and interactions with Jesus offer rich launching points into much-needed directions and considerations for our own spiritual lives. My own soul has benefited greatly from the gift of this book, and I believe yours will as well."

David C. Wang, Cliff and Joyce Penner Chair for the Formation of Emotionally Healthy Leaders and associate professor of spiritual formation and psychology at Fuller Theological Seminary

"Bruce and Carolyn Hindmarsh have a remarkable ability to combine solid biblical insight with perceptive spiritual direction. Through their gentle and loving guidance, this little treasure will help any disciple of Jesus 'be still and know' him more deeply. I will gladly keep this book close at hand for years to come. Thank you, Hindmarshes, for such a needed and nourishing gift in our fast-paced modern world."

Shawn Reese, pastor of Peninsula Bible Church Cupertino

AT THE FEET OF JESUS

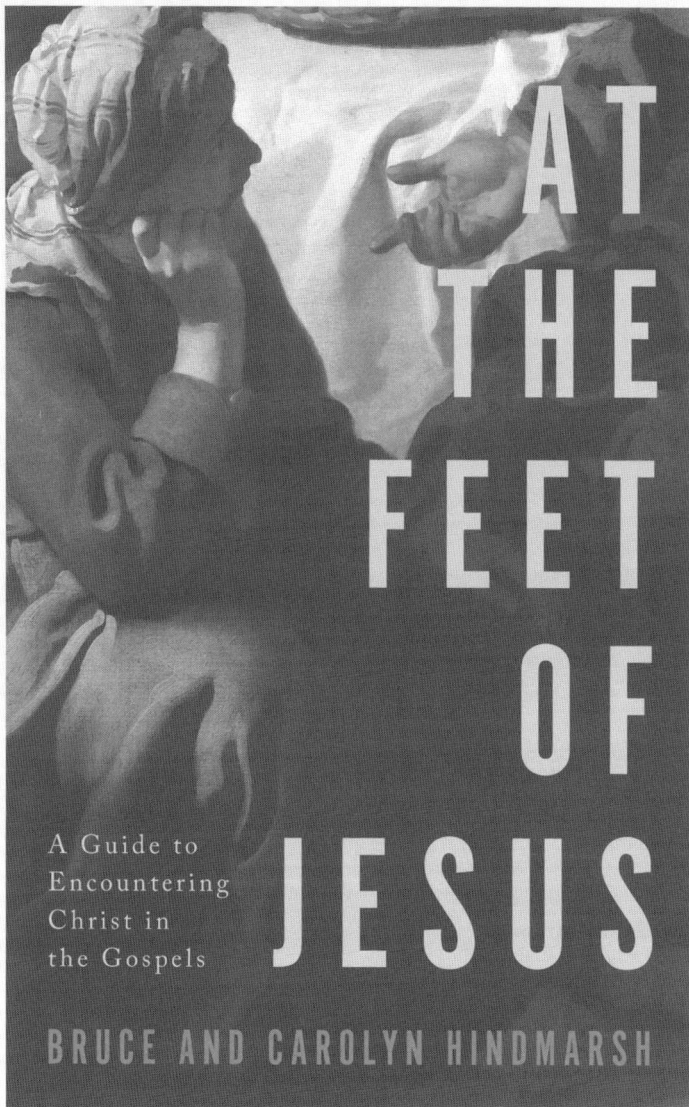

A Guide to
Encountering
Christ in
the Gospels

BRUCE AND CAROLYN HINDMARSH

≋
ivp

An imprint of InterVarsity Press
Downers Grove, Illinois

InterVarsity Press
P.O. Box 1400 | Downers Grove, IL 60515-1426
ivpress.com | email@ivpress.com

InterVarsity Press® is the publishing division of InterVarsity Christian Fellowship/USA®. For more information, visit intervarsity.org.

All Scripture quotations, unless otherwise indicated, are taken from The Holy Bible, New International Version®, NIV®. Copyright © 1973, 1978, 1984, 2011 by Biblica, Inc.™ Used by permission of Zondervan. All rights reserved worldwide. www.zondervan.com. The "NIV" and "New International Version" are trademarks registered in the United States Patent and Trademark Office by Biblica, Inc.™

While any stories in this book are true, some names and identifying information may have been changed to protect the privacy of individuals.

Published in association with the literary agency of WTA Media LLC, Franklin, Tennessee.

The publisher cannot verify the accuracy or functionality of website URLs used in this book beyond the date of publication.

Cover design: Faceout Studio
Interior design: Jeanna Wiggins
Cover image: Bridgeman Images, Image ID: Bridgeman - BBAL_68033

ISBN 978-1-5140-1053-2 (print) | ISBN 978-1-5140-1054-9 (digital)

Printed in the United States of America ∞

Library of Congress Cataloging-in-Publication Data
A catalog record for this book is available from the Library of Congress.

32   31   30   29   28   27   26   25 | 13   12   11   10   9   8   7   6   5   4   3   2   1

To Jim Houston

CONTENTS

PREFACE

It has been our privilege to lead a number of prayer and discernment retreats over the years for various groups. We have been able to stand witness to the work of the Holy Spirit in the lives of many men and women as they have read the Scriptures prayerfully in the presence of God with "all hearts open" (as the *Book of Common Prayer* says). We have often felt that we were on holy ground. On one occasion we took a small group of graduate students away on retreat at a beautiful spot on the Sunshine Coast of British Columbia near Pender Harbour. We were leading a three-session retreat on praying with Mary of Bethany (the material that would become this book). On Saturday afternoon, we sent our students off in silence to pray on their own. While they were off praying, we were praying for them—praying for the pray-ers. For a moment, it seemed as if we could see their faces turned toward God in prayer, lit up and made radiant by the face of God looking at them. Nothing could be more beautiful. We gathered again for our evening session over a meal and continued the retreat. It was a memorable weekend. The students seemed to encounter Jesus Christ in the Gospels in a way that was life changing. We are still in touch with many of them.

It was witnessing this sort of response to joining Mary of Bethany at the feet of Jesus, poring over the Scriptures in prayer, that prompted us to write this book to see if we could make this experience available to others. We are grateful to Ted Olsen and the excellent team at Inter-Varsity Press for sharing our vision and supporting the endeavor with all their expertise. It is because of them that you can hold this little book in your hands.

We have learned so much from those who have joined us on these retreats. We're more thankful than we can say for our amazing students who seem to know instinctively that study and prayer belong together. We're especially thankful to Bruce's teaching assistant Dan Glover and his wife, Trina, who became close friends as we led this retreat and cooked together for students. We want to offer special thanks to Shawn Reese and the pastoral team and congregation at Peninsula Bible Church Cupertino for inviting us many times to lead retreats, for their generous hearts and their love for the Scriptures, and for welcoming us as friends. Ian McFadden and his band of fellow pastors prayed with Mary of Bethany on Galiano Island, and it was humbling to see their raw honesty with God and with each other—and their good humor. Bishop Steve Breedlove and the clergy of the Diocese of Christ our Hope joined us on this retreat even as we were honored to watch them go on to renew their ordination vows—a moving ceremony of consecration and self-donation so much like the way Mary poured out her pint of nard at the feet of Jesus. And we owe a debt of gratitude to all the other groups that have spent time with us and Mary of Bethany at the feet of Jesus.

Over the years, our notes for this retreat have become so mixed up that we hardly remember what each of us first contributed. Our manila folder labelled "Mary of Bethany" grew and grew and got jumbled together over time. It has genuinely been a team effort.

Carolyn, an instructor in Koine Greek at Regent College, has watched her students encounter Christ in Scripture as she has led them to read the New Testament prayerfully in Greek. Yes, even in Greek! We have had Greek retreats with students in our home in the same spirit as this book. It has been her joy, increasingly, to accompany people spiritually with Scripture as a spiritual director. Her training with Dom David Foster and the Benedictines at San'Anselmo in Rome, and with Trevor Hudson and the Jesuits of South Africa and the Martin Institute, in leading the *Spiritual Exercises*, has contributed much to our retreats and to this book. This could also be said of Gary Moon and Chris Hall who, with Trevor Hudson, led the DMin program at Fuller Seminary where Carolyn trained as a spiritual director.

It would be impossible to acknowledge all the spiritual writers and biblical scholars to whom we are indebted, though we hope our notes at the back of this book point the reader to some of these sources. This book is not a work of historical-critical scholarship as such, though we hope it is informed by such work. Historical-critical scholarship is in many ways our stock-in-trade as teachers and scholars. And yet this book is doing something different than advancing contestable theses or offering historical reconstruction of first-century texts for academic debate. If we think of such work as sharpening our knives, then this book is about actually cutting some meat. As Augustine said long ago, we read the Scriptures in order to grow in love for God. We want the reader to indwell the text of Scripture rather than to instrumentalize it or *thing-ify* it. For the Scriptures themselves invite us to encounter Christ. The words of the Bible are like windows that open to allow the grace of God to enter and, like sunshine, illuminate our hearts.

So, drawing on Hans Urs von Balthasar and Timothy Gallagher in our times, and Ignatius of Loyola, Richard Baxter, and many others in times past, we ask our readers to see all the details of each Scripture passage as vividly as possible. In a way, this is a deeply human and ordinary use of our mind's eye whenever we read a novel or historical narrative. We may picture the scene to ourselves actively or passively, consciously or unconsciously, earnestly or lazily, but it is just what we do when we read or hear a story. Here, in this book, we want to get the details as realistic as possible—the clothing, the food, the buildings, the landscape, the weather, and so on—but

in the end some of this may be debatable. Who is to say whether
Martha would have served chickpeas or lamb, or whether Mary
would have worn a homespun blue tunic or something uncolored?
But it matters that we see these narratives as being as real and as
tangible as our experience of the world today. So, while we will be
speculating at points as we imagine the home of Mary, Martha, and
Lazarus in Bethany, we hope it is with an informed imagination.
We've outlined some of the theology and history of this devotional
mode of reading in our introduction, but if readers are distracted by
historical questions here and there, there are several resources to go
deeper into the details. (Consider *The Anchor Bible Dictionary* or
The IVP Bible Background Commentary by Craig S. Keener.)

This book is dedicated to Jim Houston, our teacher and friend of
many years, who has taught us in so many ways that we may never
stand aloof from the word of God but must always remain at the feet
of Jesus in faith, hope, and love.

THE DISCIPLES AT HOME

WHEN WE THINK OF JESUS AND HIS DISCIPLES, we usually think of the twelve who traveled with him in his public ministry and who were uniquely called by him and designated his apostles (Luke 6:13-16). However, we might also think of the three who were his friends and whose home he visited on at least three occasions.

When we first encounter them, we learn that "Martha opened her home to him" (Luke 10:38). We meet Martha and her sister Mary and (later) their brother Lazarus. We might think of Mary, Martha, and Lazarus, therefore, as the domestic disciples. Indeed, Jesus refers to Lazarus as "our friend Lazarus" (John 11:11), and the three are together described as uniquely beloved by him: "Jesus loved Martha and her sister and Lazarus" (John 11:5).

In this small book, we would like to help you, like Martha, to open your home to the Lord Jesus Christ and to consider what it might mean to invite him into this most intimate space. What does it mean to be befriended by Jesus Christ and beloved by him in such an interior way? We are certainly called to follow him in the world as disciples and to share in his public mission. But we are also called to receive him and allow him to enter in and make his home with us.

Jesus is still saying, as he did to the church at Laodicea, "Here I am! I stand at the door and knock. If anyone hears my voice and opens the door, I will come in and eat with that person, and they with me" (Revelation 3:20). Is there any invitation more wonderful or more sacred? How remarkable to have table fellowship with Jesus Christ, to be permitted to be his host, to welcome him, and have him for our guest!

It is at home, behind closed doors, that we dare to voice our greatest hopes and fears, that we experience our deepest joys and sorrows. It is at home that we are known most intimately and fully. In the Gospels, the Lord Jesus chose to visit Martha, Mary, and Lazarus in their ordinary home and to enter fully into their messy lives. On each occasion, his presence made all the difference.

We will consider all three domestic disciples at home in the village of Bethany, but we will focus the spotlight especially on Mary and invite you to follow her in her response to Jesus. By placing yourself there with Mary at the feet of Jesus, you can pray with Mary of Bethany and make her wholehearted response your own.

MAKING A RETREAT

We have designed this book as a prayer retreat. It can be used as a group retreat or as a personal retreat, or can simply be read through as a devotional book, but it is meant above all as an invitation to prayer and to encountering Jesus intimately for yourself. (Suggestions for how to use this book are provided in chapter one.)

It is said of the *Spiritual Exercises* of Ignatius of Loyola that you do not so much read the *Exercises* as you *make* them. So also with this retreat. In this sense, you might think of the chapters that follow like a recipe for a meal. You are meant to make the recipe, and it is in the hands-on sifting, mixing, kneading, baking, and, above all, eating that the beauty of the recipe is experienced. In a way, the recipe should fade away and eventually disappear. There is something much more than the recipe to discover. The words on the page are to be transformed into something felt, handled, touched, and experienced personally.

ENCOUNTERING JESUS

John said of Jesus Christ: "We have seen his glory" (John 1:14). He wrote of a Word "which we have heard, which we have seen with our eyes, which have looked at and our hands have touched" (1 John 1:1). This is meant to be your experience too. The invitation is to a genuine *koinonia* or fellowship "with the Father and with his Son, Jesus Christ" (1 John 1:3).

Our hope is that this small retreat might help you to deepen your personal response to Jesus. As you follow Mary of Bethany in prayer, you can encounter, with her, the presence of Christ in the midst of your real life and experience today. He comes to you in your home too.

We witness in Jesus Christ the eternal Son of God, begotten of the Father from all eternity. As he "became flesh and made his dwelling among us," so we are privileged to see in his every word and action the very heart of God (John 1:14). The disciple Philip said, "Lord, show us the Father and that will be enough for us," and Jesus replied, "Don't you know me, Philip, even after I have been among you such a long time? Anyone who has seen me has seen the Father" (John 14:8-9).

So, as we follow Jesus throughout the Gospels—as we see him heal Peter's mother-in-law, teach the multitudes on the mountain, rebuke the religious leaders in the synagogue, cleanse the temple in Jerusalem, and so on—at each and every point we are seeing heaven on earth. The implications of this are profound for us as we read the Gospels and encounter Jesus with the disciples at Bethany.

With every gesture and every utterance, Jesus mediates God to us. Heaven and earth are uniquely joined right here. This invites our close attention.

AN OPENING IN HEAVEN

This is what Nathanael discovered when he first encountered Jesus. Jesus was not only "the one Moses wrote about in the Law, and about whom the prophets also wrote" (John 1:45). He was the new Bethel, or

house of God, the place where Jacob's ladder eternally rests: "You will
see 'heaven open, and the angels of God ascending and descending on'
the Son of Man" (John 1:51; see Genesis 28:12). Here in Jesus Christ,
God made flesh, heaven stands open and will remain open forever.
Jesus is that opening in heaven even now as we open the Scriptures.

Augustine once described the Scriptures as "the face of God for
now," and he urged us to "gaze intently into it." What did he mean?

You and I were each made to see the face of God, and every
Christian heart longs to be able someday to look into the face of love
itself. Every human being was created in innocence and purity to walk
with God as in a garden. The great promise is that someday we shall
be washed, cleansed, and restored by grace; we shall be made fully
capable of this. Meanwhile, where do we look to find the face of God
turned toward us? Again, "Anyone who has seen me has seen the
Father," says Jesus (John 14:9).

We must look to Jesus. And where do we find him today? Because
"the Word was with God, and the Word was God" and because "through
him all things were made," there is nowhere in all creation that God is
not speaking, where the Word of God is not articulate (John 1:1-3).
"The heavens declare the glory of God" (Psalm 19:1). And God has
spoken in the past "at many times and in various ways" (Hebrews 1:1).
He continues to speak in nature, in history, in human experience, in
all these ways. We should always, everywhere, be listening for what
God might be saying to us. All this speech belongs to the one eternal
Word who has become human for our sake. But all these modes of
speech are still only like whispers that have now been gathered into
"the full volume of the divine voice in the world" in Jesus Christ. To
listen to Jesus, we turn to the Scriptures where he is decisively revealed.
In the union of the word written and the Word made flesh, we encounter God himself today. Here we may still find Jacob's ladder
joining heaven and earth.

This means we need to pay attention to everything about Jesus. What Jesus is doing in the Gospels *he is always doing*. Heaven is still open here in Jesus at every moment we encounter him in holy Scripture. The eternal Son of God, the risen and ascended Jesus Christ, is with us *now* as we read the Gospels today.

If he is the incarnate Word of God, the eternal Son, then he can never be simply past tense. He was there in the village of Bethany in the first century. He is here in my room now as I turn the pages of my New Testament.

By the Holy Spirit, the past and present are fused in the burning heat of God's revelation in Scripture. This is what Jesus promised in the sending of his Spirit: "I will not leave you as orphans; I will come to you" (John 14:18).

JESUS IS PRESENT NOW

This means that as you read about his visit to the home of Martha, Mary, and Lazarus—at the very moment you are reading—Jesus is as present now, as really and truly present to you, as he was to them. These were real events in time and space, a history as real as the moments we live today. Jesus was there and then. But as the eternal Son of God, he is also here and now.

When we speak a word today, the sound of it rings out for a moment and then quickly dies away and all is silent once more. A spoken word is like a word written on the sand. The wind or the waves come over it, and soon enough it disappears. It is not so with the words of Jesus Christ in the Gospels.

These words once spoken have not decayed or faded away. They have no diminishment or half-life. They continue to ring out with the same volume and intensity as when they were first spoken. There is a vernal freshness and eternal wellspring to the words of Christ in the Gospels. This is what Peter meant when he described our spiritual life as having its origin "not of perishable seed, but of imperishable, through the living and enduring word of God" (1 Peter 1:23).

Imagine ringing a bell, only to find that the sound keeps on ringing and ringing and ringing. The note once sounded just keeps on going. That is what the word of Christ in Scripture is like. No mere past tense. No antiquarian distance. It is all happening now in real time. And it is the communion of persons: Jesus is alive, and he is speaking with you.

This is why you can pray with Mary of Bethany. As you substitute yourself in the place of Mary, you will find in each encounter that the face of Jesus is turned toward you. You are being addressed personally. These words are meant for you.

SEEING THE PLACE

Sometimes we may form indistinct or hazy images in our minds as we read the Gospels. The narrative hovers in midair somewhere, as something far away and long ago. There are no crisp edges or vivid colors. We are perhaps overfamiliar with the words. Or we read more or less passively, without making the effort to see, hear, and feel what is happening, experiencing the narrative as real.

There is a danger here that we will not sense that what we are reading is *just as real* as what is happening in our day-to-day world right now.

We have both worked for many years mostly in academic contexts. But we have also done some work in the arts. Carolyn has written a play, and Bruce has worked on a film, and we have done a few other creative projects. It has been a real eye-opener, literally. These experiences have changed how we read.

Recently Bruce worked as a historical expert for a documentary film crew in Britain. They consulted him for their reenactments with surprisingly precise questions: Would John Wesley be wearing a wig in 1767? Would it be shoulder-length? What color would William Wilberforce's frock coat be when he went to meet John Newton? What tune should be used for the congregation singing "Amazing Grace" in 1773? Would they sing in a call-and-response format? Who would lead? Was there an organ?

All of a sudden, the demands of the medium asked more of his imagination than he had needed to give before, despite years of reading. The demands of the creative, artistic format made him realize that he had not fully seen or heard or felt what he had studied. His images were still gauzy and vague. This experience exposed that even his work as a historian had not gone deep enough if he had not fully imagined his subjects—picturing them vividly to himself in their context.

So, in this retreat, we will be asking you to engage your *imagination* to see, hear, and feel as vividly as possible the Gospel accounts of Mary of Bethany and her encounter with Jesus. It really happened. Everyone would have smelled the food in the kitchen. The light would have come in at an angle through the window and lit up Jesus' face as he taught. A fly might have crawled along the windowsill. Perhaps Simon Peter cleared his throat, or a cart clattered by on the cobblestones of the street outside.

We sometimes think of imagination today as make-believe or fantasy—just making things up. And this is, of course, one of the remarkable things that we human beings can do. We can imagine fauns and centaurs and aliens with three eyes, and so on. But the imagination is also employed when we close our eyes and try to re-picture to ourselves the face of someone we love, or a room from our childhood. And the better we can imagine (re-picture) these things, the more real it all feels to us.

Modern psychologists and therapists understand this connection between imagination and feeling, but so did the ancients, for whom memory was the faculty of the human mind that did all this work. It was the very deepest part of the soul. From Augustine to the late Middle Ages and beyond, Christians understood that this faculty needed to be engaged in the reading of Scripture. There were a number of "lives" of Christ during these centuries that encouraged vivid medi tation on each episode in the Gospels. Ignatius of Loyola took this up and made it central to the retreats he gave his followers. He described this kind of vivid meditation in the *Spiritual Exercises* as a "composition" or "seeing the place." Later, English Puritans encouraged a similar practice.

It seems that Christian artists understood this especially well. When Fra Angelico painted simple frescos of Dominic adoring the cross for each cell in the dormitory for the brothers at San Marco in Florence, he meant for them to see themselves in the figure of Dominic and place themselves there at the foot of the cross in meditation. Rembrandt took this even further, painting himself right into the scene of the raising of the cross of Christ.

There are vivid paintings of Christ in the home of Mary and Martha from the Spanish artist Diego Velázquez and the Dutch artist Jan Vermeer. (We used a detail from the latter for the cover of this book.) We can see these painters wrestling to imagine the details and somehow fuse the present and the past; this is a form of contemplation similar to Ignatius's "seeing the place."

What about you? Can you see the place as you read the Gospels today? The task for you with this retreat, as you contemplate Mary of Bethany, is to engage your inner senses as vividly as you can. This is not arbitrary invention. It is not so much seeing whatever you will as seeing as much as you can.

We have a friend who is slowly going blind. Each morning he sits in his chair by the living room window, looking out at the gently rising interior mountains in British Columbia. He watches as the sun comes up and the grassy slopes turn to gold against a windswept sky of cerulean blue. He told us that he is memorizing the view, so that when he loses his sight, he will still be able to picture it vividly to himself. He is really and truly training his inner senses, his memory and imagi-nation, so that he will be able still to see as much as he can.

He is also remembering: *re-membering* the scene, putting its pieces back together and holding it before his mind's eye. We do this when we want to remember loved ones who are separated by time or dis-tance. So also should we remember Jesus Christ. As Peter wrote, "Though you have not seen him, you love him; and even though you do not see him now, you believe in him and are filled with an inex-pressible and glorious joy" (1 Peter 1:8). As Christian believers, we want to remember Christ as vividly as we can.

LOVE'S PICTURE

If you are reading for edification and attentive to the Holy Spirit speaking now through God's Word, then it is love's picture that matters most: love seeking to remember the beloved. In this, commentaries and study notes and historical accounts of first-century Palestine may certainly help, but only as aids to contemplation.

The main thing is to see the place in a way so real, so immediate and sensate, that you feel pulled into the frame and absorbed into the scene. The horizon line dividing the past and present is erased. When Jesus speaks, you are the one he is addressing. You are the one who touches the hem of his garment. It is your grief when Jesus' coming seems delayed. It is your storm that must be calmed. Your bent body that must be raised upright.

We met a dear woman in her eighties who lost her loving husband after more than fifty years of marriage. She spoke of how painful it was to find in certain moments that she could no longer picture or imagine him. But then there were other moments where his presence was pro-foundly real and vivid. In these moments, she could see him so clearly in her mind's eye and hear his voice so distinctly in her mind's ear that she would almost turn and speak out loud with him. It was like she could reach out and touch him.

This is the experience that we hope you have as you engage your imagination in reading about Mary of Bethany.

One of the best accounts of such loving contemplation comes from the Swiss theologian Hans Urs von Balthasar. In fact, he turns to the relationship between the lover and the beloved to explain contemplation: "Love desires to have the beloved before its eyes. Thus the contemplative will employ the powers of his soul to summon up the image of the Beloved, the powers of his 'inner senses' and his imagination to call forth the image of the incarnate Word."

He continues, describing how the devout Bible reader does this: "He will contemplate Jesus as he dwelt bodily on the earth, the things he said, the sound of his voice, the way he treated people, his appearance when at prayer, at the Last Supper, in his Passion." But, again, this is not journalism or reportage:

> This picture is not meant to be a realistic photograph, but love's picture, solely concerned with love, the divine love of the Father, which is here manifested in the Son and in the concreteness of his whole earthly life . . . we do so in order to seek for the love of God, to see, hear and touch it in the humble form in which it offers itself to man. In prayer, our love seeks love, divine love, through the earthly image (with which it cannot dispense).

"Love seeks love," says Balthasar. "Love desires to have the beloved before its eyes." If this is something that strikes a chord in your own heart, then you are ready to go on retreat.

Throughout this retreat, you are not alone, for the gift of the Holy Spirit makes this contemplation possible. Jesus promised, "When the Advocate comes, whom I will send to you from the Father—the Spirit of truth who goes out from the Father—he will testify about me" (John 15:26). He says again: "The Spirit will receive from me what he will make known to you. . . . In a little while you will see me no more, and then after a little while you will see me" (John 16:15–16).

A PRAYER

As you enter into this guided prayer retreat, prepared to look afresh at the Lord Jesus through the eyes of Mary of Bethany, take a moment to pause and to offer up to God your own desire to draw near to Jesus and encounter him personally.

Begin first with a simple prayer to acknowledge that God is here and to place yourself in his presence. If you are doing this with others, you might use this ancient call and response:

The Lord is here.
His Spirit is with us.

This prayer acts like a reminder. Again, it is like opening the door to your home and welcoming a much-anticipated guest. If you are doing this on your own, you might use the words of Francis de Sales: "O my heart, my heart, God is truly here!"

In these prayers we not only seek to become aware of God, but also to remember that God is aware of us—looking upon us with love.

Secondly, offer up a prayer for the retreat itself. If the Lord is here, then what is your response? What do you hope for from this time in his presence? What do you want? As you take a moment to focus your intention, as you prepare for the retreat as a whole, you might pray slowly several times over these words below. This prayer is ascribed to Bishop Richard of Chichester as his dying prayer in the thirteenth century.

O most merciful Redeemer, friend and brother,
May I know you more clearly,
Love you more dearly,
Follow you more nearly. Amen.

In the first prayer, we open our hearts to the Lord who is present right now by his Spirit. And with this second prayer, we respond and ask for a specific grace from God. We are asking God in his mercy to change our hearts as we meditate on Scripture.

A STRUCTURE FOR PRAYER

To structure this retreat, we have adapted a pattern of biblical meditation and prayer that has come to us through the ages from the wisdom of the church. It is an approach that seeks to be holistic, using all
our powers. For Catholics and Protestants alike, this centuries-old
method has meant engaging our memory (and imagination), our reason, and our will. Prayerful reading of Scripture is never just brain
work. Christians have been praying out of Scripture this way for a long
time. We've provided a historical note on some of the sources for this
form of prayer, in case you would like to explore further on your own.

Here, then, is an outline of each session's structure. You can refer
back to this as you go. Think of these as five simple steps to approach
Jesus through the Scriptures in prayer. They provide a path by which
we come to him: prepare, see, reflect, respond, and review.

PREPARE

It could probably be laid down as a general rule that intimacy takes
time and thoughtful preparation.

We cannot emphasize enough how important preparation is for
each of our three sessions. Sometimes we rush into prayer breath-
lessly, as if we were showing up late for a meeting. And God must
surely have compassion on us, knowing the pressures we face and the
burdens of each day. Jesus did say, "Come to me, all you who are weary
and burdened, and I will give you rest" (Matthew 11:28). And yet. And
yet, we need help to remove these burdens and settle down into this
rest. We need to slow down into prayer.

The prayers we have already offered demonstrate the posture we
want to settle into, a way to slow down and orient ourselves as we
anticipate the retreat as a whole. We can offer these same prayers
as preparation for each session. There are some additional (time-
honored) practices to help us further prepare our hearts for each of
our sessions. Consider these as four simple ways to dispose ourselves
toward God as we approach the Scriptures. We will put some of this in

the first-person singular ("I pause to be aware . . .") to help you make this your own.

Aware of God. Here I pause to consider for a moment how God is looking upon me right now in love.

This is a deliberate recollection of the presence of God. He is here. I pause to be aware that he is with me and that he is looking upon me with love. It is as if I lift my eyes to meet his. Ignatius of Loyola used to take a moment to make an "act of presence" like this before praying over Scripture "for the space of an Our Father." How long exactly would it take someone to recite the Lord's Prayer? We don't know, but not very long. Long enough, though, to catch your breath and remember: God is here.

You might light a candle as a symbol that Christ our light is here. To remember the presence of God, consider beginning each session with a simple prayer like the one we used above:

The Lord is here.

His Spirit is with us.

Pray this slowly, and as many times as you need for it to sink in. Allow some silence for it to sink deep. We sometimes forget the things that are most true. *O my soul, God is here.*

Available to God. I offer all my will and actions to God, with nothing held back.

This naturally follows from an awareness of God's presence. I offer all that I know of myself to all that I know of God in an act of surrender. I'm not going to enter into prayer with any reserve or standoffishness. I'm not saying, "I'll wait and see what God wants before I decide whether I'll agree." I'm saying, "What you want, when you want, where you want, as you want, Lord—I'm here and I'm willing."

Again, this need not be a long or fraught prayer of preparation. I pray simply, "Here I am, Lord. I'm all yours." Balthasar calls this kind of prayer of preparation "a leap of the child into the heart of its father." The surrendered heart is a trusting heart. It matters that we are honest with ourselves and with God. Sometimes we may have little more to say than "I want to be available. I want to want you, God."

Let's use the prayer of Samuel (from the Old Testament book of 1 Samuel) for this self-offering. As we did with our earlier prayer, you may want to repeat this a few times, more slowly each time, emphasizing different words. Offer yourself as entirely available to God:

Speak, Lord, for your servant is listening.

Throughout the Scriptures, listening is linked to obedience. It would be good to leave some silence after praying these words. What better way is there to signal that we are waiting and open, listening with all our hearts for God's word and ready to obey?

Alive to God's Word. Here I preview the Scripture that I am to consider.

This is where we first turn to the passage and read it through. When our children were in piano lessons, they sometimes had to sight-read the music when learning a new piece. They looked carefully, picking out the notes on the piano, following along. We called this "getting acquainted" with the music. This is what we are doing here. Our preview of Scripture is not yet the main event; it is a chance to look over the passage in anticipation. It's a flyover, or a reconnaissance mission.

So, I preview the passage of Scripture, slowly reading and absorbing the meaning of the words and thinking about how God might meet me here. The first time I sight-read a famous piece of music by the composer Bach, I don't expect to achieve mastery. It is a time to notice, with awe and reverence and anticipation, what is set out before me. So also with Scripture. There is so much to take in, and I want to be alive to all the possibilities. By paying close attention, I begin to enter imaginatively into this Scripture passage.

In this first preview you can make an initial effort to compose the scene in your mind's eye. Remember that you will read and reread through the text multiple times; that is what close reading entails. For now, take a first look. Instead of standing back, enter in. Read actively, not passively. If you were there with Jesus and the disciples, what would you see, hear, and feel?

Asking for God's Grace. Now I ask God specifically for what I want from him in this time of prayer.

I have previewed the passage as an act of preparation, but now I pause in anticipation. Readying myself for a deeper prayerful engagement with this text of Holy Scripture, what is it I would like to ask of God? If I were to be really changed by this encounter, what would it look like?

We sometimes imagine that our emotions and desires appear out of nowhere. In reality, our desires are being molded all the time by stories, rituals, expectations, examples, and practices. A rose bush can be pruned to find its natural shape, or it can be left to run wild. Life has a corresponding form. This is true too of our life in Christ. Christ is both the source and the form of our spiritual life. We want to be more like him. In prayer we express our desire for this.

As we dispose ourselves to God's grace, real change can take place in our character and our desires.

Sometimes it feels impossible that we will ever really change. Can my fundamental desires really be turned toward God? Can I ever truly love what he loves? The great promise is that the Holy Spirit longs to use Scripture in our lives in exactly this way. In this last stage of preparation, we chime in. We *ask* God for this transformation. And we get specific. This is important. We need the help of the Holy Spirit to shed light on the words of Scripture so that we will be addressed personally. This is God's word, and it is only God who reveals God.

As you previewed the passage, you may already have found something glimmering, something speaking to you, something that touches your desire to be changed. Pay attention to this. Is there something to ask for from God? Hold onto this, since this may surface again later in your personal response to the passage.

In meditating on Scripture, we can expect that God will speak to us personally in a way that will follow the grain of the passage itself. To change the metaphor, we want to swim with the current, and certainly not against it. We look for a consonance too with the whole biblical message. In the guided reflections we are offering as we come along-side Mary of Bethany, we will be asking God by his Spirit to work in us increased faith (Luke 10), greater hope (John 11), and deeper love (John 12). These are core theological virtues. And none of this is abstract. What do we ask for? It is faith in Christ, hope in Christ, and love for Christ himself.

This preparation may look like a lot to do when you see it laid out like this in four paragraphs, but really it is a simple matter of pausing just to *remember, offer, preview,* and *ask*. These practices aim to culti-vate four dispositions in us as we make ready a space for God. We seek to be aware of his presence, available to him, alive to his every word, and utterly dependent upon his grace. And we'll guide you through the preparation for each of the sessions.

One last note: it is probably a good idea to turn off your phone notifications.

SEE

As we noted above, in earlier centuries there was a desire to meditate on Scripture with "all our powers." Reading Scripture prayerfully was not just a cognitive exercise. It meant using our memory, our reason, and our will. To remember Jesus is therefore where we begin. As we said earlier, memory and imagination belong together, just like when you close your eyes and picture the face of someone you once knew or a place you once lived. You remember. You form a picture. You imagine.

This is where our meditation proper begins. We have previewed the passage once already in our preparation, like a warm-up exercise. Now we seek to explore it in earnest, slowing down to indwell it with our inner senses. We go back through the passage a second time. We did a flyover at 36,000 feet, but now we walk through on the ground. In the sessions that follow, we will lead you through the passage in this way with our imagination. Moving through the passage, we will take time to "see the persons," to "hear the words," and to "observe the actions." We will also enter into the feelings and point of view of each of the persons. You can follow along point by point as the conversation and action in the passage progresses. Place yourself in the scene. If you were in the home of Mary, Martha, and Lazarus, along with Jesus and the disciples, you would turn and look at the one speaking. Then you would follow the conversation to turn and look at the person who responds. You would notice things. If a dish shattered, you'd hear it. If a roast was in the clay oven, you would smell it.

Here is your chance to enter into the Scriptures with your imagination and involve all your senses, your inner senses, as you read. We'll help you to do this. Sometimes we will ask you to focus on this or that person or detail. This is what will help you be really present to what Jesus is doing. This is what will help you hold the whole scene in your mind vividly, so you can go on to consider everything more carefully.

REFLECT

Having used our inner senses to enter into the biblical episode as fully and vividly as possible, we can then pause to reflect upon it all prayerfully. From our power of imagination, we turn to use our power of reason.

Don't think the use of reason means reverting to a detached analytical mode. Far from it! This too is a continuing exercise of prayer from the place of the heart. We are told that Mary, the mother of Jesus, "treasured up all these things and pondered them in her heart" (Luke 2:19, compare v. 51). We will do likewise. We remain open, pliable, and present to God. Memory, reason, and will are not separate, mechanical operations of our souls, nor do these faculties ever really work in isolation. But as the process continues, we may foreground one activity over the other.

Think of holding the scene in your imagination as if you were pausing a film at different points. You may ask yourself more about what is going on. What is Jesus doing? Why is he delayed? Why is he weeping? You may ponder the actions and words of the other actors in the story and wonder about their feelings. You may want to ask questions of yourself. Have you ever felt like that? If Jesus is here revealing what God is like, what does that mean in your own experience?

In each of the sessions that follow, we'll offer various reflections of our own for you to consider, as we look at the biblical scenes from various angles and raise questions about what is going on.

RESPOND

The most natural thing in the world follows from entering the scene with our imagination and from this kind of slow thinking over Scripture in the presence of Jesus. As the desert father John Cassian wrote, such prayerful meditation is like "every hour and every moment working over the earth of our heart with the plough of Scripture." This work brings us to a place of response.

The very Jesus who was present to the crowds, his disciples, and his friends is present with me now. We said earlier that what he does in the Gospels he is always doing. He is still offering himself in love today as he did in the Gospels. His gaze is directed toward me. I can talk to him freely, as my heart is moved. Returning to the passage therefore a third time, hovering over it and pausing here and there, I enter into conversation with Jesus: *What do I hear him saying to me? What do I want to say to him?*

You've been praying all along in this exercise, but now is the time to focus upon and deepen this conversation with the Lord. In each session, we will provide a number of prayer prompts to get you started on praying personally out of the biblical scene. It is well worth slowing down here to see if some of the questions feel especially pertinent, like they are lit up. This is a cue to linger longer and consider these things in prayer for as long as is needed.

However, you need not treat these questions like a workbook exercise to go through from top to bottom. In fact, it is quite important that you don't! It may be that in the freedom of God's Spirit there is just one of these questions you need to stay with, and you can leave the rest. Or these questions might prompt you to notice something else altogether. The Puritan Richard Baxter used to say that if you find the wind of the Spirit blowing, then you should stop and hoist the sail.

REVIEW

Before rising from the meditation to return to the rest of your day, you should ask yourself if you feel a particular emotion or call to action. Here, you are engaging the power of your will and affections. Once, when Bruce was doing one of these exercises, he felt especially moved by a deeper sense of gratitude to God. He felt called both to notice this gratitude and to be more careful about complaining, especially concerning small things. What might God be asking of you in these passages of Scripture? How might your affections and desires be moved? Are there decisions you need to make?

In the beautiful spontaneity of the Spirit, there will almost certainly be something for you—just for you—to take away. The Lord Jesus Christ sees you as uniquely as he saw Mary, Martha, and Lazarus, and he addresses you individually today. There is "a white stone with a new name written on it, known only to the one who receives it" (Revelation 2:17). Like Hagar, you can say, "You are the God who sees me" (Genesis 16:13). There is something for *you* as you sit at the feet of Jesus. See if you can notice what this is. It helps to write it down or tell someone about it, so you don't forget.

If you lit a candle as part of your preparation, now is the time to blow it out. You may want to pray quietly the words of the Lord's Prayer to conclude the session. Think of this like saying grace for a meal, but at the end.

Here is one last piece of advice—which is really just an image to keep in mind. Francis de Sales thought that after a time of prayer you should leave the place of prayer as if you were carrying a vessel full to the brim of a very precious liquid. Imagine your favorite cup of coffee or tea, filled to the top. As you go, you try not to spill anything. It is all too precious. As we step away from our prayers, we go softly, not wanting to lose a drop. Soon enough comes the rush and noise of daily life.

1

HOW TO USE THIS BOOK

IN THIS BOOK, WE GUIDE YOU through three devotional meditations on Scripture, one on each of the passages where we meet Mary of Bethany. We've written these to be used in different ways, depending on your situation.

Although we have described this book as a retreat, another helpful approach might be *to read it through on your own*, as you would a typical book, pausing to pray and consider the content and the questions raised. We've written it so you can do this if this is best for you. Perhaps you might jot down in a journal some of what seems to strike you most deeply or write your own prayers there in response.

Another approach would be to use these three meditations on Scripture *for a guided personal retreat*. To do this, you should set aside some dedicated time. You might set aside a block of time for three mornings in a row, or perhaps three Sundays in a row. It could also be very meaningful to take a weekend for a private retreat, even going away somewhere on your own. This approach allows you to go through each meditation on Scripture slowly, at your own pace. In this context, you could pause as long as you needed for prayer and reflection, re-reading sections, and carrying on a natural, prayerful conversation with God about your own life and what he might be saying to you right now.

Using this book for a personal retreat is especially fitting if you are in a time of discernment about a major decision or carrying a particular burden for yourself or someone you love. What better place could there be to put these concerns than at the feet of Jesus?

Lastly, though, we have also written this book to be used as *a multi-person retreat,* whether for a couple, a few close Christian friends, a small group, a leadership team, or a larger weekend retreat for a church or Christian organization. In this context, you can think of the three Scripture meditations as three sessions. We have led this retreat with many such groups in the past.

How should you use this book for groups? If you are the leader of a *small group* or want to do this retreat with friends, it might be easiest if each person has a copy of the book. This allows you to configure your time together with minimal formality. You can let the book structure your sessions. Having time to go for walks and eat together allows the experience to be unrushed. Ideally, you'd be able to go away for a weekend together; otherwise, you could take a day retreat at a suitable location. The sessions can begin with everyone gathered for worship, but then people can go off individually to work through the meditations, returning after a period to debrief together and share insights with the others. You can close each session by giving time for folks to offer up short prayers that arise from the meditations on Scripture. Over the course of the retreat, seek to balance private meditation with shared conversation and fellowship.

There are a couple of ways this could work for *a larger group retreat* with more formal structure. We suggest that the retreat leader study the book and use it to develop the three sessions as a guided retreat. The meditations on Scripture in this book can be adapted for the leader like a script to fit your setting. You might want to print out the "Respond" questions for each section to provide prompts for people to use for their own time of quiet after the group meetings. Having copies of the book to send home with people for their own further reflection is a way to extend the significance of the retreat and allow people to revisit its themes on their own.

We suggest two possible schedules for a large group weekend retreat.

Schedule One: Sometimes people are rushing away from work and arriving late on a Friday for a retreat. If this is the case for your group, you can use Friday evening simply as a preview time of worship and welcome. Then the sessions could be spaced out for Saturday morning (Luke 10), Saturday evening (John 11), and Sunday morning (John 12). On this schedule, it is good to allow for an unhurried time on Saturday evening to explore the experience of suffering and loss in John 11. We have found that this session can sometimes expose more tender areas of our lives where, like Martha and Mary, we are asking, "Where were you, Lord?"

Schedule Two: If your group is ready to start on Friday, you can study Luke 10 on Friday evening, John 11 on Saturday morning, and John 12 on Saturday evening. Sunday morning can include a service to offer up the whole experience in worship (perhaps including the Lord's Supper) and a time of sharing. On this schedule, Saturday evening (John 12) ought to be a time of joy in the presence of Jesus, just as the family of siblings rejoiced over a meal after Lazarus had been returned to them alive. It is a time for consecration, pouring out our love at the feet of Jesus, but it is also a celebration. We have sometimes done this session over a real feast. Once we made beef bourguignon for our students on a Saturday evening and led the whole meditation right there at the table while having dessert and coffee.

You can of course rework the material to fit other schedules. Whatever your retreat context, use the "Structure for Prayer," outlined in the introduction, to allow the retreat to proceed and flow naturally.

2

FIRST MEDITATION

Sitting at Jesus' Feet in Faith

LUKE 10:38-42

As Jesus and his disciples were on their way, he came to a village where a woman named Martha opened her home to him. She had a sister called Mary, who sat at the Lord's feet listening to what he said. But Martha was distracted by all the preparations that had to be made. She came to him and asked, "Lord, don't you care that my sister has left me to do the work by myself? Tell her to help me!"

"Martha, Martha," the Lord answered, "you are worried and upset about many things, but few things are needed—or indeed only one. Mary has chosen what is better, and it will not be taken away from her."

PREPARE

Let's take a few moments to prepare to meditate on this passage. (If necessary, go back over the section above in the introduction on "A Structure for Prayer" and review the steps outlined there to be *aware* of God's presence and to make yourself *available* to God; to be *alive* to God's word and to *ask* for his grace.)

Aware of God

The Lord is here.

His Spirit is with us.

Available to God

Speak, Lord, for your servant is listening.

Alive to God's Word (preview the passage)

Now, we can take time to preview this Scripture together—to get acquainted with the text. Take a moment to read slowly over the passage.

This passage from the Gospel of Luke takes us to the first recorded encounter of Jesus with his friends in the village of Bethany. Jesus is in the midst of his public ministry and teaching, after he has "resolutely set out for Jerusalem" from the northern Galilee region (Luke 9:51). The crowds have begun to thin. He has begun to speak of his coming suffering and the cost of following him.

He enters an unnamed village where "a woman named Martha opened her home to him." We know from later accounts that this was the village named Bethany on the east side of the Mount of Olives, about two miles from Jerusalem (John 11:1). For most people, this walk from the city would take about forty minutes. Later, as the end approached ("six days before the Passover") and as the events of Jesus' passion unfolded, Jesus would return to this village and lodge there with his disciples (John 12:1; Mark 11:11; Matthew 21:17; Luke 19:29).

We are not told whether this is the first meeting of Jesus with this family, but the first person we meet is a woman named Martha noted for her hospitality. She opens her home to Jesus. (Luke describes it specifically as *her* home.)

The home is a fitting place for Jesus. He not only engages fishermen and tax collectors in the marketplace, calling them to follow him and share in his ministry, but he also enters into the intimate sphere of home, family, and close relationships. He belongs here.

He stands ready to be present in your home even if your home isn't what others might consider ideal or ready. This home is described as Martha's home even though Lazarus apparently lived there too, making such a description unusual for the time. Why is it called *her* home? Was Martha a widow? Had she inherited the home from a late husband? Was she taking care of Lazarus and Mary? Why are these siblings' parents missing?

It seems possible that there was a history of grief and loss for this family at Bethany, possible that Martha, Mary, and Lazarus had experienced the death of those close to them. It seems there had been tears in this home—as in all of our homes.

As you prepare to invite Jesus into your own home, as you retreat for a while, turning away from your busy life and public responsibilities, shedding your professional roles, you may be aware that opening your home to Jesus means more than just opening a door. You too have a history, a backstory of your own joys and sorrows. Sooner or later, early or late in life, we all learn that the world is not as it should be. For all the goodness and abundance of God's world, it remains at present a vale of tears, and few of us get very far without some sorrow, suffering, and loss. No one gets out alive.

So, whether you are happily married or happily single, whether you are struggling in your marriage or struggling with parenthood or struggling in your singleness, it does not matter. You don't have to have a perfect Instagram family to welcome Jesus. There can be something amiss, and there can be problems.

At Martha's invitation, Jesus has stepped under the lintel and over the threshold to be fully present in this home with all its family history.

Let us deepen our awareness of the presence of Jesus by echoing the hospitality of Martha, who has welcomed Jesus into her home.

Jesus stands ready to enter your home. Take a moment of silence and recollection, and then pray, simply, "Jesus, you are welcome here."

Thinking about the fullness of what this means, pray over this a few more times more slowly. Pause between each repetition, emphasizing in turn one of each of those five words as you pray.

We've read over the passage and begun to dwell in it. We are ready to spend some time in the village of Bethany and meet Mary and her siblings. Taking our place there alongside this family, we may find our response to Jesus in theirs.

It is striking that in each of the passages where we encounter Mary of Bethany, her position is always at the feet of Jesus. We see her sitting at Jesus' feet (Luke 10), falling at Jesus' feet (John 11), and finally anointing Jesus' feet (John 12). This is a movement of deepening prostration and devotion: sitting at the feet of Jesus and listening with rapt attention (faith), falling in bewildered grief at the feet of Jesus when all hope is lost (hope), and then anointing the feet of Jesus in entire devotion, holding nothing back (love).

In this session we will take a closer look at this first movement: sitting with Mary of Bethany at Jesus' feet in faith.

Asking for God's grace. Having previewed this passage, let us remember to ask for God's grace. We do not make this retreat with our own strength. As you offer up this time of prayer and reflection on God's word, considering the visit of our Lord to the home of Martha and Mary, what do you feel you need? Thinking of this particular scene, you might ask that Christ would increase your faith. "Lord Jesus, increase my faith."

Having acknowledged our need for grace and called upon God for his help, let's return to the Gospel scene and enter more deeply with our imagination.

SEE

To see the place is to be like a painter or photographer who looks carefully at the visual elements that will compose the picture. Ignatius reminds us that when we are contemplating Christ our Lord, we are contemplating one "who is visible." This is a simple, but easily overlooked, corollary of the incarnation—God in human flesh—and it invites us to look intently.

Let's do this with our passage from Luke 10:38-42.

We have five verses, comprised of just ninety words in the Greek text. Join us as we place ourselves in Martha's home. To see the place involves not only sight, but all the other senses too. Using all your senses, try to see, hear, feel, even smell what is described.

Let's try picturing it.

∽

Imagine a band of travelers in Palestine on a dusty road in the hot, late afternoon. They have walked some eighteen miles up the steep, winding path from Jericho and the Jordan valley toward Jerusalem. There are beads of sweat lining their faces and necks as they arrive in a small village on the eastern side of the Mount of Olives. They have climbed almost three thousand feet across rocky desert terrain. They are relieved to find a warm welcome in the small village of Bethany. A woman named Martha has opened her home to them. Imagine you are right there with them.

It is an ordinary home shared by three siblings. There is a courtyard with a few chickens, and pens for goats and sheep. You can hear the chickens clucking and the sheep bleating as you arrive. There is a pungent earthy smell as you draw closer. The house has sturdy stone walls, covered in mud plaster bleached white by the sun; above is a flat roof used for storage and sleeping on hot nights, accessible from a staircase outside.

You enter the main room on the ground floor. There seems to be just enough room for everyone, though it is snug. The dirt floor, strewn with straw, is tidy. There are some storage chests, woven baskets with dried fruits and vegetables, and a trestle table. There are pegs on the wall by the door for cloaks and satchels. You can see some smaller adjoining rooms to the side and behind for storage and sleeping.

Just now, the wooden shutters are open on a window, and evening light filters in from the west. Dust motes dance in a sunbeam, and the room has a warm, golden glow. You see a stone hearth on the wall to your right connecting to a covered kitchen with its walls partly open to the courtyard that wraps around to the east. You glimpse an earthen oven, a stone lid to a sunken cistern, several large clay pots, more baskets scattered about, and another trestle table laden with produce.

After a basin of water is brought and the travelers' feet are washed, they settle on the cushions scattered along two walls of the main room. A few sit on the long, low bench beside the table. You look around. There are Peter, James, and John, along with Thaddeus, Andrew, Nathaniel, Thomas, and the rest. At least fourteen people are crowded into this room, but all are turned toward Jesus. He is sitting on a stool by the window. Having rested for a little while, he has now begun to teach and to tell stories about the kingdom of God.

As you look closer, you see that Martha's younger sister Mary is there, closest to Jesus, sitting with the men, listening with rapt attention. The men are mostly wearing simple, undyed tunics, tied at the waist. Mary stands out with her pale blue shawl worn over her tunic, her long hair hanging in a single braid down her back. Her face is radiant, lit up not only by the sunlight but by her inner joy as she listens to Jesus, lovingly attending to every word. It is though time stands still and Jesus is the only thing in the world that matters to her.

Meanwhile, Martha has been thinking about how to feed all these people. Her hair is tied back, and she has an apron over her linen tunic.

She has run out to call on the neighbors to borrow some additional clay goblets and plates. The dinnerware is lined up on a board in the kitchen. A shoulder of lamb is roasting on the fire. The smell of rosemary and garlic is beginning to filter into the main room.

Now, with mortar and pestle, Martha vigorously crushes chickpeas and garlic, pouring olive oil little by little from a small clay jar, adding sesame-seed paste and a little salt to make hummus for the flatbread that is baking on the clay bricks on one side of the oven. There is a platter of sliced cucumbers and peppers, and a bowl of dates, figs, and nuts. Fish fillets are frying in oil in a pan, seasoned with dill. A pot suspended above an open fire has boiling water ready for lentils. Some larger clay pots lie half buried in dirt and straw, keeping water and wine cool. Martha loves Jesus too, and she wants to give him and his friends a great meal.

But it's not just the water that's simmering. Martha keeps glancing over to the main room, where the dreamy Mary has once again lost track of time and responsibility. Mary has once again left her to do all the work. Martha moves too fast and drops a serving dish. You can hear it shatter, and you can see that Martha's emotions have shattered too. Everyone is suddenly quiet. Martha turns abruptly toward Jesus, unable even to look Mary in the eye: "Lord, don't you care that my sister has left me to do the work by myself? Tell her to help me."

This is an awkward moment, and everyone can feel the tension. Mary's head is downcast now, eyes on the floor.

Look, though, at the face of Jesus, and see the tenderness as he turns and addresses Martha by name. She is not unseen or unnamed by Jesus. He says her name twice. Maybe she is so overwrought, he needs first to get her attention: "Martha." And then, after a pause for her to turn and really look at him and hear him, he speaks her name again, more quietly: "Martha. You are worried about many things"—maybe he gestures to all the dishes she is preparing, all the chaos in the kitchen—"but only one thing is needed." And then he defends Mary against her sister's resentment: "Mary has chosen the better part, and it will not be taken away from her."

∾

What was this like for you? Could you see the place and experience all that was going on in this house at Bethany as if you were there?

Before we go on to reflect on this scene, take a minute just to enter into the emotions in this scene. Let us observe not only the actions of the persons but also what it seems they are feeling. What are the sibling dynamics? Write down what you think Martha and Mary might each have been feeling. Can you relate to this? What do you think the disciples themselves were feeling at different moments in this scene— arriving, settling in, witnessing a family argument, and so on?

Do you instinctively identify more with one of the sisters as you do this? People sometimes say, "I am more of a Martha," or "I am more of a Mary." Be careful with these reactions. Try not to think of this passage as a personality test, as if these two sisters are symbols of introversion and extraversion (the Jungian personality types). While the sisters had their own personalities, the account of Mary and Martha is not about personality types. This is not a first-century Myers-Briggs quiz or an Enneagram exercise. There is a Mary and a Martha in each one of us.

The only real question is whether you are keeping your eye on Jesus, no matter your personality.

REFLECT

We have held the scene in our imaginations and fixed it there. Now we reflect further upon the scene. We think about what is going on. We ask questions and mull things over, pondering these things in our hearts.

First, consider this scene in terms of the customs that governed roles and relationships between men and women in first-century

Palestine and the ancient world. Rabbis generally did not include women among their disciples and would not teach them. Mary seems to have been doing something unconventional, if not a little scandalous, by joining the men who gathered around this rabbi.

Was Mary challenging traditional norms by taking a place at the feet of Jesus with his disciples, listening to his *logos*, his teaching? Whatever the situation, Jesus clearly considered her a disciple, and he authorized her presence at his teaching publicly, in the presence of all, and against any objections. Jesus had a particular regard for women which Luke notices and emphasizes in his Gospel.

What about you? Is there any way that you have felt excluded from Jesus and his community because of social norms or culture? If there are any scolding voices that you have internalized that make you feel like an outsider, then you might want to read over this passage again from this perspective and hear Jesus' defense of Mary, in the presence of all, as his authorization of you. By replacing Mary's name with your own in the final verse, you can personalize the words of Jesus. *You* are welcome to sit at his feet. You get a front-row seat.

Second, take a moment to consider the scene practically. Maybe you've had a dinner party where your preparations became way too complicated and you were frazzled as the guests arrived. You made four or five appetizers and had pots on the stove, dishes in the oven, and all manner of vegetables lined up and ready for the next prep stage when your friends arrived, and so on. (Sometimes, our meals feel like they require military-grade time-and-motion studies.) After your guests have left, have you ever realized that you got so preoccupied with the preparations that you were not able to focus properly on these special people? Might it have been better to serve soup and bread and to pay close and loving attention to each one around the table?

When we think of the scene in these practical terms, we realize that Jesus may well have pointed to all the bustle in the kitchen when he said, "You are worried about many things." A less work-intensive meal might have been fine, rather than an attempt to serve "many things." A simple focus on Jesus might have called for a more simple meal.

There is a reminder here that true hospitality is always about self-giving and not self-display. There is nothing wrong with hosting a big, special meal (as we shall see in John 12). Feasting is not only deeply human; it is a sign of the kingdom. One day we will all celebrate the wedding supper of the Lamb. Moreover, cooking is often an expression of love. All this work is to be offered up to Jesus and done in his presence. But if we cannot also give loving attention to our guests, then we may need to simplify the plan or prepare in advance to avoid too much fuss at the end.

In the midst of her anxious serving, Martha missed the opportunity to pay loving attention to Jesus and learn from his teaching. Elsewhere, Jesus says that what we do unto the least of his brothers and sisters we do unto him: "I was hungry and you gave me something to eat, I was thirsty and you gave me something to drink" (Matthew 25:35). Jesus is present in the person of our guest. We miss out if we are so preoccupied with our work of serving that we cannot focus attention on the guests we are serving. We too might be missing an opportunity to attend to Jesus himself.

There is another twist to this story. Sometimes, we can be preoccupied with seemingly spiritual things in such a rigid way that we miss a calling to hospitality right in front of us. We might be tempted to point to Mary when we are dreamy and oblivious to the needs of others. As we will see next, prayer and service belong together. What matters is keeping one's eyes on Jesus.

Third, pressing more deeply, we can step back and consider the scene in its literary setting in the Gospel of Luke. What comes before? What comes after? We can rewind the film a bit, and then fast-forward a bit, to consider where we are in the story here.

The scene preceding is the parable of the good Samaritan, responding to the question, "Who is my neighbor?" (Luke 10:29). A priest and a Levite pass by the man who had been beaten and robbed, but a Samaritan stops to bind up his wounds and care for him. He demonstrates real neighborly love.

In the scene following our passage, the disciples see Jesus at prayer, and they ask him, "Lord, teach us to pray." They want to get in on what they see him doing. In response, Jesus teaches them a form of prayer that we know today as the Lord's Prayer.

Our passage comes between these two scenes: between love of neighbor and love of God. It is like the hinge that joins the two, the glue that binds them. In the Gospel of Matthew, Jesus taught that the first and greatest commandment was "Love the Lord your God with all your heart and with all your soul and with all your mind." And the second was like it, "Love your neighbor as yourself" (Matthew 22:37-39).

Where do you think this teaching comes in the Gospel of Luke? That's right: It comes just before we reach Bethany. So it all progresses like this: First, Jesus teaches on love of God and neighbor. Next, he tells the story of the good Samaritan. Then, he visits the home of Martha and Mary. Finally, he teaches his disciples the Lord's Prayer.

When you look at it this way, it is clear that our passage is the meat in the middle of the sandwich. It is positioned between love of neighbor and love of God; between service and prayer; between the active life and the contemplative life; between acts of mercy and acts of piety.

In the modern world, we can so easily live without a prayer. Life in this context reinforces an attitude that says, "It all depends on me": I exist as a resourceful agent acting on the world. As you and I go about our day-to-day lives in the twenty-first century, we are receiving a kind of catechism about what it is to be a human being. We can move around rapidly wherever we want and communicate instantly to whomever we want. We carry a supercomputer in our pocket much more powerful than the Apollo astronauts could have imagined. We make consumer choices constantly. The message in all of this, and in many other daily practices, is that we are immensely resourceful and capable.

No wonder we can go for hours and hours literally without a prayer, even when we seek to serve in Christ's name. We don't remember that we need God until life goes really sideways.

This attitude of "agent resourcefulness" creates a serious danger for the Christian who would seek to serve Christ: engaging in all kinds of prayerless activism. We begin serving spiritual food we haven't tasted. In contrast, all the great classics of pastoral theology in church history speak with one voice: spiritual self-care is the first task of anyone who would seek to serve Christ. One's contemplation of Christ is the first thing. *This* is the one thing necessary. Out of this one thing flows a life of consecrated service.

Bernard of Clairvaux was a remarkable spiritual writer and influential Christian leader of the twelfth century. Here was a man of deep prayer and active service—a Mary called to the life of Martha. Bernard had an arresting metaphor for how all this works together. He said he wanted to be a reservoir rather than a conduit. A reservoir fills up to the brim, and if it overflows, it does so without losing any of its fullness. In contrast, a conduit is empty and only passes on the water it receives; then, it is empty again.

As teachers and parents, we've often felt like conduits. But Bernard's image has helped each of us pray to be more like a reservoir.

A Roman fountain with its nested bowls works like a series of reservoirs. The fountain fills the topmost, smallest bowl, which overflows to the next, larger bowl, which in turn fills and overflows to the next, largest bowl. Each bowl loses none of its fullness in passing on its surplus.

Take a moment to consider personally how the rhythms of work and prayer flow together in your own life. What God has joined together, let no man put asunder. Our actions in the service of others must take place without losing sight of Jesus. We keep our eyes on him.

Our service is not in our own strength; it flows from prayer. Where in your own life do you see the need to knit together prayer and service more closely?

Fourth, we might consider this passage from the point of view of a philosopher. Since the dawn of philosophy in Greece, thinkers have considered the question of the One and the Many. Is there an underlying unity in the multiplicity of the world? What holds it all together? Even the quest in physics today for a grand unified theory to account for the fundamental physical forces of the universe is a continuation of this problem. How does everything hang together?

In our world of rapid change, it seems as though everything comes to us in fragments, like data packets without context. Pluralism, globalization, technology, digital communication—all these conditions have uprooted us from identity-giving traditions and communities. And it can be terribly confusing. One sociologist describes our experience today as "liquid modernity."

Yet as the book of Colossians says of Jesus Christ, "He is before *all things*, and in him *all things* hold together" (Colossians 1:17, emphasis added). Indeed, Paul says "all things" six times in this context in Colossians (verses 15-20). By the time you get to the end of Colossians, it is clear that this same Christ is meant to be at the center of *all things* of our lives: "And *whatever* you do, whether in word or deed, do it *all* in the name of the Lord Jesus, giving thanks to God the Father through him" (Colossians 3:17, emphasis added).

Like the ordinary English words *one* and *many*, the Greek words in our passage in Luke are common, everyday words: Martha was distracted with "many" things, but only "one" thing was necessary. And yet. Christians in time past could not resist seeing something more going on here, something symbolic. Surely, to contemplate Jesus rightly is to see that he is the answer to this ancient problem of discerning the unity underlying a world of change.

Here, in Jesus Christ, is the Archimedean point of the universe. Here is the center of the turning wheel. As Dante wrote at the pinnacle of the *Divine Comedy*, the love of Christ is the "Love that moves the sun and all the other stars." Mary saw the "one"; Martha saw the "many things." Martha somehow couldn't see the one right before her in whom all things hold together.

Mary could see the unity; Martha was lost in the multiplicity. Note that this is not simply philosophical. It is about love. Jesus Christ is the culmination of all our desires. All laborious activity is temporal; only love will last into eternity. Christ is the fulfillment of all our loves. What Mary had chosen would "not be taken away," said Jesus. In 1 Corinthians 13, it is clear that all sorts of gifts will pass away, but love will endure forever.

From the earliest times Christians have thought long and hard about Mary and Martha. Building on the reflections of philosophers, it wasn't long until they took Mary and Martha as symbols for the contemplative life and the active life. For St. Augustine, these women symbolized the present and the future, the laborious and the quiet, the troubled and the happy, the temporal and the eternal, knowledge and wisdom, and so on. Indeed, Mary and Martha have figured largely in such reflection since the earliest days of the church to the present.

There is a splendid artistic example in France. We visited Chartres Cathedral some years ago and were awestruck by the sculpture and stained glass, all this poetry in stone and glass created in the twelfth and thirteenth centuries. Viewed from above, the building is laid out like a cross. As you approach from the west on foot, if you turn left and walk around the front of the building, you come to the north porch which makes one end of the transept, or the horizontal bar of the cross. And there, if you look up at the entrance, you will find Mary and Martha in stone.

The outer ribs of the porch above the entrance—what are called the archivolts—are decorated with ascending female figures on the left and the right. One is doing textile work with wool; the other is opening a book and praying. One is Martha; one is Mary. The active life of service; the contemplative life of prayer.

But what makes this symbolism so profound for us is that these figures meet at the top. Together they frame the entrance to the presence of God, represented by the interior of the cathedral itself. Prayer and work belong together as we seek the presence of the Lord. It is all about keeping our focus on him.

Jesus was not demeaning service but warning against distraction. In sixteenth-century Spain, Teresa of Avila told her sisters in the Carmelite order not to consider the greatness of the work they do, but rather the love with which it is done. She also told them, rather whimsically, that we must make friends of Mary and Martha. We must unite them to show proper hospitality to the Lord:

> Believe me, Mary and Martha must join together to show hospitality to the Lord and have him always present and not to host him badly by failing to give him something to eat. How would Mary, always seated at his feet, provide him with food if her sister did not help her? His food is that in every way possible we draw souls that they may be saved and praise Him always.

In a different vein, many theologians in the past also noticed that the gap between Martha and Mary represented a kind of necessary progression in the spiritual life. The gap was between temporal distractions and the attainment of love, and this seemed to signify the nature of the Christian life as growing in love. As we leave behind anxious striving in our Christian experience, we enter more into peace and rest in God. It is like you row the boat first, with much labor, and finally get it out into the wind. Then you can hoist the sail and put down your oars. Love takes over.

There is a lovely essay by C. S. Lewis on "first" and "second" things. He argues that making second things a first priority results in losing not only the first things that you are neglecting, but also those very second things that have become your preoccupation. The man who makes work his whole life loses not only his family and friends but also, in the end, the proper pleasure of work itself. Lewis states the general rule this way: "Every preference of a small good to a great, or a partial good to a total good, involves the loss of the small or partial good for which the sacrifice was made."

This leads naturally to the one and only question of crucial importance: What things are first? As Lewis rightly says, this question "is of concern not only to philosophers but to everyone." Loving attention to Jesus must always be the first thing.

Our passage of Scripture calls us to a singularity of focus on Jesus, whatever we are doing. This is the first thing, the one thing that is necessary. How different this is from the singularity of resentment: Mary has left me to do the work *alone* (Greek *monos*). We are called from the singularity of resentment ("Woe is me") to the singularity of devotion ("Great is he"). That's our focus.

Fifth, it is worth pausing to consider the psychological dynamics that show up in our passage. Let's think about the scene from this angle. There are three really big emotional words in Greek associated with Martha in these five verses. Martha was *distracted*. Martha was *worried*. Martha was *upset*.

Distracted is a word occurring only here in the New Testament. It means to be divided, pulled apart, busy, and overburdened. Can you relate to those emotions in your own experience? With our modern world's constant demands on our time and attention, distraction seems to have become the norm. Consider the pull of our smartphones, which were designed by the smartest and wealthiest people in the world to distract us and hold our attention. I might be sitting in the same room with you, but my attention to my phone means: *Not here, not now*, and *not you.*

For some of us, time management itself has become, as David Allen says, a kind of martial art. The inbox will never be empty. The to-do list will never be finished. We are run ragged. We should pause and feel the force of this emotional word for Martha's condition: *distracted*.

It is important to emphasize again that Jesus was not demeaning service, but he was warning against the dangers of distraction. Martha was distracted with "much serving." Jesus wants our undivided attention. In fact, the word in our passage for *distracted* was used by Paul in 1 Corinthians 7:35 in the negative (*undistracted*) to describe the sort of devotion he wanted family members to give to the Lord. Give him your *undistracted* attention.

Sometimes we may get too familiar with Jesus—so close every day that we miss, like Martha, the trembling awe of the one whose presence we are actually experiencing here. Jesus enters our domestic world, but we dare not domesticate him.

More significant, though, than all the calls on our attention that distract us, we must admit that it isn't just overfamiliarity or just the smartphone notifications and the pressure of our schedules that are the problem. There is something in our hearts that keeps us in the shallows. Beneath the understandable distractions of our lives there can sometimes be a more serious, or even sinful, condition. It seems that beneath Martha's spiritual distractedness was something darker in her bitterness and resentment at being left alone to do all the work. What is there in our own hearts that keeps us from sitting with Mary at the feet of Jesus?

Jesus also says that Martha was *worried*. This is the word for anxiety. It also means "not trusting." It is the word Jesus used in the Sermon on the Mount for worrying about material needs—what you will eat or drink or what you will wear (Matthew 6:25). There Jesus redirected his listeners to trust in the goodness of his heavenly Father, who feeds the birds and clothes the lilies of the field and knows just what we need. We can trust him.

Sitting at the feet of Jesus, Mary demonstrated this trust. This was enough. Jesus would be enough. There was nowhere else she needed to be. Any future concerns could wait. She was in the here and now with Jesus. And her peace of mind is in stark contrast to the state of mind of her sister.

We know with certainty that Jesus cares for those with anxiety disorders today. And for some, this is much more crippling than Martha's experience at Bethany. Maybe you are among this number. Perhaps you've experienced panic attacks and moments when it feels like you can't breathe. Jesus, the healer of the sick, has compassion for all those who suffer in this way, even as he did for Martha. Perhaps you can hear him say to you to come sit at his feet for a while and rest. "Come to me, all you who are weary and burdened, and I will give you rest" (Matthew 11:28).

The third big emotional word used of Martha is *upset*. This word suggests being deeply disturbed and bothered. Actually, this is the same word you'd reach for to describe an outright riot. Clearly, a lot is going on inside Martha. There is no peace here. Jesus knows that for our mental well-being, we need simplicity of focus. He invites us to be mindful—mindful of him. "Take my yoke upon you and learn from me, for I am gentle and humble in heart, and you will find rest for your souls" (Matthew 11:29).

The popularity today of mindfulness as a strategy for sustaining mental health in a frenetic world is understandable, and there is much practical wisdom in the concern to slow down and be present to ourselves, to our bodies, and to what is going on right now around us. But much that passes for mindfulness today has a kind of impersonal quality to it: emptying the mind, attending to our breathing, or focusing only on the present moment. This is a good beginning, but it can be like seeing the empty chair and not the sitter. As Christians, this can only be preliminary to our mindfulness of Jesus Christ. To him we direct our attention. At his feet we find true rest for our souls.

One final consideration: we might ask ourselves whether it is really lack of faith, ultimately, that keeps us from sitting at the feet of Jesus. Everything else is so much more immediate. It is hard to trust, really trust, that listening to Jesus is the most important thing in the world. We need our faith to be strengthened. It is faith that trusts Jesus has the words of life, that here is what is first and best. We need the Holy Spirit to increase our faith, as we prayed earlier. Above all, we need to look intently at Jesus in the Gospels and see afresh that he is always and everywhere enough. He is still the one who calms the storm, heals the sick, comforts the afflicted, and offers to all the word of life. He is enough.

Life is indeed busy and full of distractions. But it is clearly not simply busyness that keeps us from Jesus. Busyness is often just moral laziness. It is time to lay aside, once and for all, the excuse that we are too busy to sit with Mary at Jesus' feet. We decided some years ago not ever to say how busy we are. We have just as much time as everyone else. Talking about how busy we are can come across as way too self-important, like a signal to others of how valuable our time is. No one needs an epitaph on his tombstone that says: "At least he was always really busy."

What is really keeping us from Jesus? It isn't just that we are busy.

There is a lovely poem by one of our former students, Heather Kaufmann, entitled simply "Martha." The form of the poem itself is like a long, vertical, psychological descent, sinking beneath the waves of our distracted lives. Indeed, the central imagery is of water ("I am a sea of distractions") with its cresting, foaming, and churning, its whirlwind and tempest.

But who was it that calmed the sea? And whose Spirit hovered over the archetypal chaos? The invitation at the end of the poem is "to stop," "to step," and "to listen so attentively" that we see in the holy presence of Christ that the churning sea is now calm. The question at the end of the poem is a question for you and for us all: "What would it take?"

Martha
by Heather Kaufmann
Luke 10:38-42

I am a sea
of distractions
and you
a floating island
in my midst
tossed about
by the tasks
and torrents
of the day
incessant
in their cresting
these foaming
indignities
these depths
of dreams
unplumbed

I am vast
in my capacity
to wind up
in a whirlwind
of water
and weed
above the sea
a salty encircling
tempest, filled
with the detritus
of the churning deep

What would it take to stop

                    to step
foot on the floating island
of your presence   to listen
so attentively I fail
to see the sea about me
now calm and the Spirit now
hovering over the deep?

RESPOND

We've prepared ourselves by offering up this meditation on Scripture to God at the outset. We've entered the scene of this Scripture with our senses to see, hear, and feel the actions. And we've paused to consider it prayerfully from several points of view. Now, we are ready to respond personally in prayer. Now is the time to pray with Mary of Bethany yourself. What do you want to say to Christ, as you take your place beside Mary at his feet? What do you think he wants to say to you?

We have imagined the scene together, but you can return to this now yourself, bringing your own inner senses again to bear on all the details of the passage to hold it there while you pray. Read the passage one more time, but this time imagine yourself in the scene. You are there. Substitute yourself for Mary or one of the other figures in the story—Martha, or one of the disciples observing the scene, or even that quiet character Lazarus.

Notice where you are responding emotionally to what is happening. What phrases or words seem to be leaving a mark? These may be invitations to prayer. Here below are a few questions that might lead to a personal conversation with God, based on this passage as you dwell there. As you look over these questions, stay with the ones that seem to stand out to you. It may be that something else altogether surfaces for you. If so, this is a sign to stop and pay attention.

- Jesus had friends at Bethany, and Martha "opened her home to him." What would it look like for you to show hospitality to Jesus and welcome him into your life and your home? What would it mean to show friendship to him? What do you want to say to Jesus about this?

- What in your life could be distracting you from the presence and gifts of Jesus, just as Martha was busy with preparations? What are some of the "many things" that worry and upset you? Are there any ways even in preparing and working *for* Jesus that you have been distracted *from* him? What does Jesus say to you about this?

- Martha went to Jesus with her resentment, rather than keeping it pent-up inside. Have you ever felt exasperated with Jesus like Martha, saying, "Lord, don't you care?" Can you trace the movement in your own life from busyness to exasperation to resentment? If you find yourself in this same situation, where it seems like you are all on your own ("by myself," said Martha), what would you like to say to Jesus? What would he say to you?

- Place yourself with Martha in the passage, and imagine it is you in this dialogue. Can you hear the Lord Jesus call you by name? Substitute your name when he says, "Martha, Martha." Can you listen to this gentle rebuke and invitation to be still?

- Notice Mary now, sitting at the feet of Jesus with rapt attention. What is she feeling and thinking? Try to take your place beside her and listen to Jesus. What is he saying? Can you trust that this is enough, to be here and to listen to him? What do you want to say to Jesus as you sit at his feet?

- Listening to Jesus is the "one thing" necessary among the "many things." Listening to Jesus and his word is "better" than the "many things." This will outlast the "many things." Can you take some time quietly now to worship and adore Jesus, to see something of the beauty of his presence that Mary saw? What would it look like to offer Jesus this loving contemplation, this rapt attention, in the midst of your own busy life? What would help you to keep this focus in your day-to-day life?

REVIEW

Before concluding this time of prayer, ask yourself whether anything particular lit up for you as you prayed. Go back and review your meditation. Take a look at your notes. Is there something simple but important? Pay some attention to this. Is there any invitation from Jesus that has emerged? Take a few moments to write down any insights, decisions, or new directions prompted by your meditation on Jesus in the home of Mary and Martha. Is there something for you to do?

We began earlier with the prayer "Lord Jesus, increase my faith." When we think of inviting Christ to enter our ordinary homes, as we have done, consider using the following prayer from Augustine's *Confessions*. It is so realistic about our need for grace. We used to pray it with our children when they were little. We can pray it now as an expression of faith.

> My soul is like a house, small for you to enter, but I pray you to enlarge it. It is in ruins, but I ask you to remake it. It contains much that you will not be pleased to see: this I know and do not hide. But who is to rid it of these things? There is no one but you.

When you are ready, you might want to conclude this session by gathering up your meditation and offering it to God in the words of the Lord's Prayer or some other closing prayer such as the doxology. Remember not to rush this transition. The Lord's Prayer and doxology are deeply Trinitarian, reminding us that we are offering all these prayers to the Father, through the Son, and by the Spirit. If you lit a candle to begin, now is the time to blow it out, with gratitude for the light of Christ's presence.

.

3

SECOND MEDITATION

Falling at Jesus' Feet in Hope

JOHN 11:17-44

The Meeting with Martha

On his arrival, Jesus found that Lazarus had already been in the tomb for four days. Now Bethany was less than two miles from Jerusalem, and many Jews had come to Martha and Mary to comfort them in the loss of their brother. When Martha heard that Jesus was coming, she went out to meet him, but Mary stayed at home.

"Lord," Martha said to Jesus, "if you had been here, my brother would not have died. But I know that even now God will give you whatever you ask."

Jesus said to her, "Your brother will rise again."

Martha answered, "I know he will rise again in the resurrection at the last day."

Jesus said to her, "I am the resurrection and the life. The one who believes in me will live, even though they die; and whoever lives by believing in me will never die. Do you believe this?"

"Yes, Lord," she replied, "I believe that you are the Messiah, the Son of God, who is to come into the world."

The Meeting with Mary

After she had said this, she went back and called her sister Mary aside. "The Teacher is here," she said, "and is asking for you." When Mary heard this, she got up quickly and went to him. Now Jesus had not yet entered the village, but was still at the place where Martha had met him. When the Jews who had been with Mary in the house, comforting her, noticed how quickly she got up and went out, they followed her, supposing she was going to the tomb to mourn there.

When Mary reached the place where Jesus was and saw him, she fell at his feet and said, "Lord, if you had been here, my brother would not have died."

When Jesus saw her weeping, and the Jews who had come along with her also weeping, he was deeply moved in spirit and troubled. "Where have you laid him?" he asked.

"Come and see, Lord," they replied.

Jesus wept.

Then the Jews said, "See how he loved him!"

But some of them said, "Could not he who opened the eyes of the blind man have kept this man from dying?"

The Meeting with Lazarus

Jesus, once more deeply moved, came to the tomb. It was a cave with a stone laid across the entrance. "Take away the stone," he said.

"But, Lord," said Martha, the sister of the dead man, "by this time there is a bad odor, for he has been there four days."

Then Jesus said, "Did I not tell you that if you believe, you will see the glory of God?"

So they took away the stone. Then Jesus looked up and said, "Father, I thank you that you have heard me. I knew that you always hear me, but I said this for the benefit of the people standing here, that they may believe that you sent me."

When he had said this, Jesus called in a loud voice, "Lazarus, come out!" The dead man came out, his hands and feet wrapped with strips of linen, and a cloth around his face.

Jesus said to them, "Take off the grave clothes and let him go."

PREPARE

Let us take a few moments again to prepare to meditate on this new passage. (Feel free to review our preparatory steps by rereading the section after the introduction, "A Structure for Prayer.")

Let us begin with prayer.

Aware of God

The Lord is here.
His Spirit is with us.

Available to God

Speak, Lord, for your servant is listening.

Alive to God's Word (preview the passage)

Take a few moments to get acquainted with the passage. Read over it slowly in a first pass to become familiar with the words, the persons, the setting, and the actions.

We are ready to preview this Scripture together. In this passage we return to the world of Martha, Mary, and Lazarus, but it is a much more tumultuous scene. John takes some twenty-eight verses (and more, if you count the prologue and the aftermath) to tell the story; our previous passage from Luke 10 consisted of just five verses.

In this text, we find that sometimes it isn't distractions that keep us from drawing near to Jesus, but the blinding pain of suffering.

Notice that now the home is the scene not of a meal and a domestic quarrel, but of anguish, tears, and searing grief. One of the dominant notes in the mood of the passage is bewilderment: bewilderment on the part of Martha, Mary, and others that Jesus did not act sooner to save his friend. There is an old tradition, and a strong modern scholarly opinion, that the word "Bethany" might actually mean something like "house of affliction" or "house of poverty." Whatever the precise derivation of the word, Bethany had certainly become on this occasion a place of deep affliction.

Jesus' patient compassion for the confusion and grief of his very human disciples is profound, and we should sit with this for a while before rushing on to the climax of the passage. We need to let the story unfold slowly, in stages.

We are again in the village of Bethany at the home of Martha. There is a larger cast of characters this time, and the action moves outside of the house. We can picture a road leading to the village, going by the house, and on to the tomb beyond. We will be following the women as they go out of the house to meet Jesus. We will have a close view of the main characters—Martha, Mary, Lazarus, and Jesus—since these four figures are at the center of the drama. We will also see a series of intimate one-on-one encounters as each sibling meets with Jesus personally. We will notice intense emotions on the face of each one. The emotional landscape is as important as the physical landscape.

But several groups of people swirl around these four central figures. We did not print the first sixteen verses of the chapter above, but you may want to look these up for yourself. There you will see the disciples, including an early cameo of Thomas, somewhere outside of Judea. In the middle of the action, we will be introduced to a crowd of mourners at Bethany; after our passage ends, we will meet a hostile gathering of Pharisees and other religious leaders discussing the fallout. You might want to read about their plot to kill Jesus in verses 45-57.

In this first look at the passage, taking in its prologue and epilogue, we become aware of the heightened emotions and high stakes for everyone involved. This scene is also a climactic one in John's Gospel, since it is the seventh and last *sign* (the word John uses for Jesus' miracles) and the most dramatic. The passage is full of tension, unexpected turns, dramatic irony, a slow reveal, and a big, big ending. There is so much to take in.

We have divided this passage, as Frederick Dale Bruner does in his commentary, into three meetings of Jesus, one with each sibling. Jesus meets with Martha. Jesus meets with Mary. Jesus meets with Lazarus. Each meeting is intimate and personal. We will return in a moment to enter the scene in more detail. But as you preview the passage, do you have any intuition already of something important for you?

Asking for God's grace. Before we meditate on this passage further, let's do as we did previously and ask God for what we want from this encounter with Jesus in the Gospels. In the scene in Luke 10, we noticed that Mary sat at Jesus' feet in faith. Now, in this passage, in heart-rending grief, she falls at Jesus' feet. Where else do we turn when all hope is lost?

We invite you to pray quietly, alongside Mary of Bethany, for the grace of hope: "Lord, strengthen my hope." If you find yourself in a dark place with little hope at all—just a tiny, sputtering flame—you may need to pray with even deeper urgency: "Lord, *restore* my hope."

SEE AND REFLECT

In the previous meditation, we imagined the scene with you before reflecting on it (as we will do with our final passage). For this longer passage, however, we will combine our seeing the place with our reflection on the scene. First, take a few moments to read over the passage again on your own. Go more slowly this time, taking in each meeting. Pay close attention with your senses to the action, especially the shifting emotional experiences and reactions. Watch each of the main characters carefully. What do you see? What do you hear? Even, at one point, what do you smell?

The story opens in the first verses of John 11, with Lazarus seriously sick. The sisters send Jesus an emergency message. They don't just say that Lazarus is in trouble, they tell Jesus—or maybe remind him—that he loves Lazarus: "The one you love is sick" (11:3). They must be thinking, *Never mind the nameless, faceless crowds and the figures who come out of the shadows to beg for a healing miracle.* Of course, Jesus loves those people too; but for Mary and Martha, this is personal. *Jesus, we need you. Come and help!*

Again, Lazarus is someone Jesus loves. The narrator tells us this twice, once through the sisters, and the second time as an aside— saying "Jesus loved Martha and her sister and Lazarus" (11:5). This detail doesn't strictly need to be added, but the author wants to make sure we don't miss it.

It is easy to imagine the confidence Mary and Martha feel when they send their message: *Jesus will come. Jesus will heal. All will be well.*

Maybe Jesus is down the road, way down around Jericho, or in the Judean desert, or beyond the Jordan where John the Baptist spent so much time. Maybe he is up in Galilee. We may be sure he is continuing his remarkable ministry. But here is the first unexpected turn: Jesus seems to ignore the message that Lazarus is sick, and he stays in place for two days after the word arrives. (The disciples are just as happy to stay put, since the area around Jerusalem has become hostile territory and they aren't eager to return.) Then, in complete command of the whole situation, Jesus suddenly announces that they are going back (11:7).

John tells us that Jesus knows this sickness is for God's glory and that it heralds the beginning of Jesus' own glorification (11:4). In the book of John, *glory* is always about Jesus' path to the cross and through death to victory. Jesus is in complete control of the timing, as he is in the timing of all things in our own lives. He knows that the time is *now*, and he is ready to return to Judea to inaugurate the events leading to his passion. He is on the way to the cross when he begins to climb the steep path to the village of Bethany.

He tells his disciples that Lazarus is asleep, but they are literal-minded and don't get it (11:11). *Uh, sleep—that's good, right? When you're sick, you should sleep more.* Jesus has to tell them plainly that Lazarus is dead—stone-cold dead (11:14).

So, it's back to Jerusalem and Bethany again: back into hostile territory, much to the disciples' dismay. It isn't always easy to see what Jesus is up to. Most of us can identify with the way the disciples can't help questioning Jesus' purpose and wisdom. Is he sure about this? Why would he want to jeopardize his own mission by putting himself in danger?

Here is where Thomas, ever the Eeyore and Puddleglum of the Gospels, gets his one line: "Let us also go, that we may die with him" (11:16).

By the time Jesus and his disciples arrive, Lazarus has been in the ground for four days, so it must have been something like a week since the emergency message had been sent. You might wonder what that week was like for Mary and Martha. Surely it had been exhausting to care for their brother and watch him weaken day by day.

We don't know exactly what Lazarus's condition was, but perhaps he was tubercular: consumptive, coughing up blood, wheezing, unable to keep down any food. The sisters probably took it in shifts to sit and wait with him through the night. But we can imagine that they kept going out to the road to look toward the distant horizon to see if Jesus was coming—maybe several times a day. No messengers, no letters, nothing. Silence.

As Lazarus declined, so did their hopes. Then with a death rattle he breathed his last, and his pale body grew cold and still. It was over. And the sisters were left in stunned disbelief. How could this happen? Jesus was their friend. They had seen what he could do. They were sure he loved them too. Surely this wasn't happening. Did they cycle through at least some of the stages of grief: denial, anger, bargaining, depression?

Try to picture Martha and Mary now. Can you see their downcast eyes, their bodies slumped over and exhausted? Maybe Mary has buried her head in her hands. Observe closely their feelings. See their pacing, back and forth, and notice their vacant facial expressions. Hear their anguished sobs that come like waves.

Now, finally, there is a dot on the horizon. The word comes that Jesus is arriving at last. There is a crowd of Jewish mourners at the house, so the only place for a private conversation with Jesus is outside. Martha goes out to meet Jesus, but Mary stays home. Why? Is Mary too depressed, too disappointed with Jesus, too heartbroken to mount the energy, unsure she would even know what to say? Whatever the case, her grief is deep and overwhelming.

The meeting with Martha. Martha, the first to meet Jesus, opens with the same words that Mary will use a little later: "Lord, if you had been here, my brother would not have died" (11:21). She has had many days and long hours to think about what her first words would be to Jesus. This is what is bottled up inside her. *Where were you? You could have healed my brother. I don't understand.*

Have you ever felt this way? *God, what are you doing? Why have you allowed this to happen? If you had just been here, things would have gone differently.*

Nevertheless, Martha shows some glimmers of hope here. "Even now," she says, "I know that God will give you whatever you ask" (11:22).

What do you think she means? What is she hoping for? We don't know that she expects there to be an immediate physical resurrection of her brother. She will later worry about rolling the stone away due to the smell. It seems she has some kind of remote but real hope. Can you hear the resignation, the weariness, the sadness in her voice? Maybe what she expects from Jesus is empathy and comfort, or just a continuation of his remarkable ministry despite the huge hole left in their lives.

To Jesus' promise that Lazarus would be raised up, she says: "Yes, yes, I know, on the last day." It doesn't seem she is expecting a miracle. Martha is exercising faith, but she has a remote hope of a distant future comfort. It is as if she is saying, "The final hope is all very well and good, and thank you for that, but oh, Jesus, I just want my brother back."

Then, Jesus gently redirects her attention. Perhaps we should imagine that he looks her in the eyes directly as he makes one of the most important I AM statements in the Gospel of John: "I, Martha," he declares, "*I* am the resurrection and the life. The one who believes in me will live, even though they die" (11:25, emphasis added).

It is an electric moment. And in the next verse, he makes a very strong statement of emphatic negation in the original Greek (11:26). It is like saying, "The one who believes in me will certainly not die. EVER. Do you get this?"

"Yes, yes, I get it," she says. Then Martha goes on to make the highest statement yet affirming Jesus' identity in the Gospel of John: "You are the Christ, the Son of God, who was to come into the world." Amazing! This is the equivalent of Peter's confession at Caesarea Philippi: "You are the Messiah, the Son of the living God" (Matthew 16:16).

Somehow, in the midst of her inconsolable loss, she is able to really look at Jesus and see something of who he is. This is not the distracted Martha in the kitchen, worried about many things. Suffering has cleared all that away. She looks at Jesus and sees that he is the Christ, the Son of God, who was to come into the world. The hopes and fears of all the years are met here as Martha catches a glimpse of Jesus' true glory.

This all happens *before* Lazarus is raised. Martha is changed by her encounter with Jesus.

The meeting with Mary. Now we follow Martha back down the road to the house, where she brings a message to Mary: Jesus is here and asking for her by name. Jesus doesn't scold Mary; he simply invites her to come.

People grieve so differently. It seems that Jesus knows how hard it is to have hope sometimes. Our text says that when Mary hears this, she gets up quickly. This could also be translated as "she was instantly raised"—and that's the same verb used for the raising of Lazarus (John 12:1) and of Jesus himself (Matthew 28:6; Mark 16:6; Luke 24:6). At one level this is just like the ordinary word "raised" that we use in English. But still, Mary is *raised*. We might think of this as a mini-resurrection within the story of the larger resurrection. Mary is raised out of her depression and brought back to life in the presence of Jesus.

At the word of Jesus, at his invitation, we too can be raised out of our sorrows and emotional prisons. He offers his presence to us, even when we are at our lowest. He calls you by name and sends for you.

So Mary, ever the spontaneous one carrying her heart on her sleeve, gets up quickly and goes out. The mourners are probably thinking, *Here she goes again, grief-stricken, off to the tomb to shed more tears. Poor Mary.* This story has no shortage of spectacle, and the mourners are about to get even more.

They follow her to Jesus. Many of these followers will witness the raising of Lazarus and will come to faith in Jesus (11:45). As Frederick Dale Bruner says, this is a good reminder that when we turn to Jesus in our suffering, others are drawn to follow, like moths to a flame. They too might come to see Jesus.

Now she *falls* at Jesus' feet. She is not sitting, but falling; she is consumed by bewilderment, confusion, and anguish. She says the same thing as Martha (no doubt they had been talking): "Lord, if you had been here, my brother would not have died" (11:32). But there is a subtle difference. You should underline the word "my": *my* brother. The Greek pronoun is placed out of its normal position, up front and at a distance from the word "brother." A really tortured and exact rendering would be something like this: "If you had been here, the *of-me* would have not died brother." (Word order can get really creative in an inflected language like Greek!) But, of course, that doesn't translate as well as just underlining the English word *my*, since in the Greek this was just a way for the author to highlight the possessive pronoun. It is a special emphasis. It seems like Mary is saying, "I thought you loved me. This was *my* brother. This was personal. Jesus, I don't understand why you let this happen."

This is heart-wrenching. Have you ever been disappointed in God? The disorienting power of searing loss and crushing disappointment can shake us to the roots. Focus again for a few moments on Mary of Bethany. Imagine what it is like to be her. What is she feeling?

Now notice what she does. She falls at Jesus' feet. She is acting like Peter a few chapters earlier. When the going got tough and the crowds began to leave, Jesus asked if the disciples were going to leave him too. Peter said no: "To whom shall we go? You have the words of eternal life" (John 6:68).

Sometimes, that's all we can say. Where else, Lord? Here is where we wait in suffering: at the feet of Jesus. Like Peter. Like Mary of Bethany. Sometimes we wait flat on our face, tasting the dirt that is mingled with our tears. We don't understand, but the promise remains: the promise of life and of seeing his glory and his beauty. He who promised is faithful. "I am the resurrection and the life," says our Lord Jesus. That is still a promise we can take to the bank. The key again is to keep paying attention to Jesus. What is he doing?

Mary could have turned about sharply and walked off in anger and resentment. Instead, she falls at Jesus' feet.

So also for us. Sometimes it is all we can do to cry out with the psalmist, "Out of the depths I cry to you, LORD; Lord, hear my voice" (Psalm 130:1-2). Out of the depths of misery we cry to the depths of mercy. Where else can we turn?

> I wait for the LORD, my whole being waits,
>   and in his word I put my hope.
> I wait for the Lord
>   more than watchmen wait for the morning,
>   more than watchmen wait for the morning. (Psalm 130:5-6)

We don't just cry. We cry to the Lord.

It may have been hard for Mary to trust again after being hurt and disappointed. Maybe her own grief was a great gravestone blinding her to what God was doing. She would have missed it all if she had stayed at home depressed and not come when Jesus called her to himself. We can imagine that it took a certain amount of courage to come to Jesus and stay at his feet.

We cannot overstate how intense the emotions are in this scene—and not just Mary's emotions. The narrator says that Jesus is "deeply moved in spirit and troubled" (11:33). That last word "troubled" is a big one. It suggests real inner turmoil and agitation, like calm waters being stirred up into a rough sea. But the first word, translated "deeply moved in spirit," is even stronger. This word, unique in the New Testament, suggests profound anger. It is a word used elsewhere in ancient literature for horses that are snorting and chafing at the bit, bristling and bracing themselves for a battle to come. They are stamping and ready to rush upon the enemy. It seems that Jesus is indignant, fuming at death itself. He is angry with the powers of darkness. He is ready to assault the realm of Satan and to rescue all who are under the power of death and suffering.

He asks, genuinely, in his humanity, "Where have you laid him?" (11:34). Then comes the shortest verse in the Bible, one that tells us of Jesus' heartbreak: "Jesus wept" (11:35). There was a cascade of tears. For the third time, we hear of Jesus' love for Lazarus: "See how he loved him!" (11:36).

How good it is to know that we do not have a remote God who cannot be moved by our suffering or by the worst horrors of the human condition. Jesus knows he will raise Lazarus, but still he weeps. The man of sorrows, acquainted with grief, enters into our experience of loss and bewilderment. He weeps.

It is a good reminder that all our suffering can be assimilated to the suffering of Christ. Our tears can be mixed with his. There is room enough in the sacred heart of Jesus for all the sorrows of the world. Where else can we turn? We fall at his feet, knowing that here alone is the first and last hope of the world.

The meeting with Lazarus. But Jesus does more than weep. For the second time, we are told that Jesus is moved. He proceeds to demonstrate his absolute authority.

An unstoppable force meets an immoveable object as Jesus confronts death. Martha is worried about the smell that might come from her brother's corpse, but Jesus reminds her of his promise. Again, John points out that the glory of God is on display in Jesus' confrontation with death and his victory. "Did I not tell you that if you believe, you will see the glory of God?" says Jesus (11:40). With great authority and at full volume, Jesus shouts three words: "Lazarus!" "Come!" "Out!"

And with a certain amount of bathos, Lazarus stumbles out of the tomb—still wrapped up in his grave clothes. Life, not death, has the final word when Jesus is around.

As we said earlier, John uses the word *signs* to describe these miracles of Jesus, including this climactic miracle. All of these signs pointed to Jesus' identity as the Son of God and Savior of the world. And all of these signs would culminate in the "book of glory" in the

Gospel of John: the account of Jesus' own suffering, death, and trium-
phant resurrection. It is this Jesus who is the hope of the world and
our hope.

That's why we fall at his feet in hope, even when we are utterly dev-
astated by inconsolable loss. It is for this that we have Jesus.

It is clear that God's plan for the salvation of the world was not for
everyone to get a miracle as the sisters did here when they received
their brother alive. This was a sign of the kingdom, not God's strategy
for saving the world. There are still signs of the kingdom all around us
today, and we may still ask in compassion and faith for such signs, but
all these signs only point us to Jesus as the hope of the world. You don't
spend time looking at a signpost; you get on the road in the direction
it is pointing. Jesus is the destination. He is making all things new, and
his reign has begun.

But this means, of course, that not everyone in Israel was healed. In
fact, Lazarus had to die a second time. Have you ever considered that?
What was that like for him? Perhaps he thought, "Oh no, not this
again!" Or, much more likely, perhaps he faced his second death with
a solid hope and confidence, knowing personally what it meant to
trust in Jesus as the resurrection and the life.

Carolyn has had her own Lazarus experience. Her younger sister,
Nancy, had a brain injury some years ago. We prayed for her for many
weeks as she hovered between life and death in a coma. The doctors
thought all hope was gone. But after almost exactly forty days and forty
nights, like a miracle, we received her back again. She opened her eyes.
Against all odds, we got her back. She was our own Lazarus, returned
to her family in joy.

But then, nine and a half years later, Nancy died—just as Lazarus
must have done a second time. Another accident, another fall, another
coma, and she was gone. Carolyn lost her dearly beloved sister, and
the grief was intense. We all attended Nancy's funeral with a mixture
of gratitude for those nine years and acute pain in reckoning with the

loss. Yet it was in genuine Christian hope that she was laid to rest to await the great day of resurrection. Christ is raised, the firstfruits (1 Corinthians 15:20).

C. S. Lewis wrote a poignant poem reflecting on Lazarus's experience of having to come back to mortal life to face his death once more. The twelve-line poem is one long question from Stephen (traditionally considered the first martyr) to Lazarus; the question rolls on like the lines of poetry. Stephen wonders if he really was the first martyr, given that it was Lazarus who, safe in harbor, free from all harms, had to put out to sea once more. Was I really the first martyr, says Stephen to Lazarus, when you, "well knowing that your death (in vain / Died once) must all be died again?"

In death, as in life, our one focus must be on Jesus Christ. He is the resurrection and the life, and he still asks us as he asked Martha: "Do you believe this?"

The Heidelberg Catechism is a Reformed catechism from the sixteenth century—a time that knew much of suffering and death, not least from war and deadly plague. Where were Christians to look for consolation? The catechism sets one of the greatest foundation stones in all theology. With manifest pastoral concern, its authors direct us to where our true hope is found.

It begins with a question for the one being catechized:

"What is your only comfort in life and in death?"

And then it invites the answer:

"That I am not my own, but belong—body and soul, in life and in death—to my faithful Savior, Jesus Christ."

That statement is an affirmation that could be repeated every day in a spirit of prayer. It is a good confession of faith to declare after reading John 11.

RESPOND

After our prayerful walk through this passage of Scripture, we are once more ready to respond personally to God.

Read the passage again, slowly. It is a long passage, but don't rush through it. Enter into the scene once more in your imagination. Place yourself there. Look out through the eyes of this or that character. What do you want to say to Christ as you fall at his feet alongside Mary of Bethany? What do you think he wants to say to you?

Again, pay special attention to whatever stands out to you as you go through this passage. Some of the questions below may prompt you to pray over something in your own experience or a memory of loss that is still deeply felt. You may also feel impressed to pray for someone you love. Other questions might help guide you into a personal conversation with God. You don't need to work through them all. See what is most helpful.

- Sometimes distractions keep us from discerning the presence of Jesus. At other times suffering blinds us in crisis. Where is Jesus in this? Have you, or has someone you love, felt that Jesus was too late to help? That he did not show up when he was needed? "Lord, if you had been here, my brother would not have died." What comes to mind when you contemplate the sisters' disappointment? As you sit with these feelings, what would you like to say to God about this in prayer? What do you sense he wants to say back?

- Sometimes, like Martha, we have the right answer ("I know he will rise again") but we miss the presence of Jesus himself ("I am the resurrection and the life"). Can you hear Jesus saying to you, as to Martha, "Do you believe this?" Substitute your own name for Martha's: "_____, do you believe this?" What do you want to say to Jesus in response? What would it mean for you to live out of this hope in the person of Jesus?

- Hear Jesus asking for you by name in your sorrow, as he did Mary, wanting to raise you up to come to him. This was Mary's mini-resurrection. Maybe it can be yours. You can go back to verse 28 and add your name. "The Teacher is here . . . and he is asking for you, _____."

- In the pain and bewilderment of suffering, we do not just sit patiently at Jesus' feet listening. Instead, we fall at his feet in tears. Imagine yourself for a moment in the place of Mary. In the midst of your own suffering, you can fall at the feet of Jesus and express honestly your own emotional confusion and disappointment. What are you prompted to say?

- See Jesus asking about your problems with compassion, deeply moved and troubled by the pain of the world, by your pain. Hear him ask where you have laid your griefs and hear yourself inviting him to come and see. See him weeping tears over your sorrow. Can you see him nearby—not as a distant God, but a God who sees and cares and enters into your suffering? He went to the cross to bear your sin and your suffering. What do you want to say in response? What is he saying to you? How does this change your perspective on your own sorrows?

- In a sermon on this passage, Augustine suggested another possibility: "Let us hear and rise again," he said. "How many are there in this audience who are crushed under the weighty stone of sinful habits?" Augustine knew that sin and death were connected. Not all our suffering is innocent, even if it still invites compassion. If this speaks to your condition, you might offer a confession of sin and picture its crushing weight removed by Christ. You can walk free, like Lazarus, fully forgiven by Jesus.

- See the stone, *your* stone, being rolled away. Hear the voice of Jesus calling not quietly, but loudly, "Lazarus! Come out!" See the grave clothes coming off. This miracle is a sign that Jesus himself is our life and resurrection. Jesus himself is our hope. He alone has conquered death and transformed suffering into real joy. What might it mean to live out this hope in the midst of your own situation? With your mind and heart situated right there at the grave where Lazarus emerged alive again, take some time for conversation with God.

REVIEW

Before concluding your exercise of prayer, take some time to be quiet and to ask yourself whether anything particularly stood out to you as you prayed. Is there anything else that the Lord might want to say to you? Continuing in conversation with God, take a few moments to write down any insights, decisions, or new directions prompted by your meditation on Jesus' encounter with Mary and Martha and Lazarus in this Scripture. Is there anything in particular God is calling you to do?

And is there a stone you still need to have rolled away? What is keeping you, or perhaps someone you love, from experiencing the living hope of the resurrection? Is it death, or loss, or grief, or disappointment? Or something else? What would it look like for your stone to be rolled away?

Earlier we prayed, "Lord, strengthen my hope." As you look back over this meditation, you might give thanks for the times you have encountered Jesus as the resurrection and the life, your "only comfort in life and death." When you are ready, you might want to conclude this session by gathering it all up and offering it to God in the words of the Lord's Prayer, or some other closing prayer such as the doxology. It would also be fitting to use the words of the Easter greeting:

The Lord is risen.

Alleluia! He is risen indeed.

If your candle is still burning, blowing it out can be a moment of gratitude that the risen Christ has been with you.

4

THIRD MEDITATION

Anointing Jesus' Feet in Love

JOHN 12:1-8

Six days before the Passover, Jesus came to Bethany, where Lazarus lived, whom Jesus had raised from the dead. Here a dinner was given in Jesus' honor. Martha served, while Lazarus was among those reclining at the table with him. Then Mary took about a pint of pure nard, an expensive perfume; she poured it on Jesus' feet and wiped his feet with her hair. And the house was filled with the fragrance of the perfume.

But one of his disciples, Judas Iscariot, who was later to betray him, objected, "Why wasn't this perfume sold and the money given to the poor? It was worth a year's wages." He did not say this because he cared about the poor but because he was a thief; as keeper of the money bag, he used to help himself to what was put into it.

"Leave her alone," Jesus replied. "It was intended that she should save this perfume for the day of my burial. You will always have the poor among you, but you will not always have me."

PREPARE

Hopefully by now you have a sense of the simple progression of prayers in which we slow down and pause before rushing into our passage of Scripture. Let us take a few moments again to prepare for our meditation on this final text. (You can always return to the section at the end of the introduction if you need a refresher on the steps.)

Let us begin with prayer.

Aware of God

The Lord is here.
His Spirit is with us.

Available to God

Speak, Lord, for your servant is listening.

Alive to God's Word (preview the passage)

Take a few moments to get acquainted with the passage. Read over it slowly in a first pass to become familiar with the words, the persons, the setting, and the actions.

This episode was evidently very important for the Gospel writers. The anointing of Jesus is narrated in various ways in all four Gospels (Matthew 26, Mark 14, Luke 7), though only John names Mary as the woman. For Matthew, Mark, and John, this anointing forms an important part of the passion narrative leading up to Jesus' death. It is as if Jesus is being anointed for his burial ahead of time. This is not just a standalone story. It is the beginning of the final act.

Sometimes we wait until a loved one is gone to make a lavish gesture or a memorial. Mary did it beforehand, as if she could see it coming.

Take a few minutes to get acquainted with the passage, paying attention to each of the persons and what happens. Notice Lazarus, Martha, Mary, and Jesus. Notice also the disciples and Judas. Read slowly over the text and follow the action, trying to see the scene, hear the words and sounds, feel the sensations and emotions, and even smell the fragrance that fills the room. Maybe you can hear the coins clinking in the leather money bag. There is much here to observe with our senses, even just in overview.

Still, we are only previewing the text in prayer as a matter of preparation. Jesus is present with us now, the same Jesus we witness in this scene, and we want to encounter him in these words. The horizon of the text needs to merge with our horizon. We need to be pulled into the world of the text. So, we take time to read deliberately and vividly and to pause over the details. Move slowly from the meal to the anointing to the betrayal to Jesus' final words.

You will probably notice that the story has two linked halves, like a positive and negative charge: the costly gift and the calculating betrayal. Indeed, we feel a deep tension at the heart of the story here. Perhaps you can feel the social awkwardness as well as the underlying opposition. In the presence of Jesus there can be no neutrality.

Do you have some sense already of how God might meet you in this text?

Asking for God's grace. We need God's help to explore this passage in prayer. Reading Scripture can never be just a technique. If Scripture is "the face of God for now," as Augustine wrote, it is only by the Holy Spirit that we are enabled to gaze deeply into it and encounter the living God.

What do we most want from this last encounter with Jesus in the home of Martha, Mary, and Lazarus? In the scene in Luke 10, we noticed that Mary sat at Jesus' feet in faith. In John 11, she falls at Jesus' feet in hope. Here in John 12, she anoints Jesus' feet in love. She has progressed in a deeper and deeper prostration at the feet of Jesus. She has modeled faith, hope, and love—the theological virtues. As a fitting climax to her discipleship, she pours out all her love.

We invite you to pray quietly alongside Mary of Bethany for the grace to love Jesus as she does: "Lord, deepen my love." Wouldn't it be a tremendous thing if in this session you find deeper reservoirs of love for Christ opening in your own heart as you follow Mary in your affections? It is the work of the Spirit to shine a spotlight on Christ and make him beautiful to us, worthy of all our love. "Come Holy Spirit, fill the hearts of your people. Kindle in us the fire of your love."

Again, we ask simply: "Lord, deepen my love."

SEE

What do you imagine the meal was? Go ahead and imagine the different dishes, since this was clearly a real feast and, well, it was real food. We won't get it exactly right, but it is better to imagine real food than a meal in the abstract.

Remember, we will never get it precisely correct in terms of historical-critical realism, but that's not the goal here. Our imaginations should be historically informed; but more importantly, we need to feel that it *really happened* on a certain day, at a certain time, in a certain place, with certain people. Without the senses, lost in abstraction, we aren't really there. We stay detached. By using the furniture of your own mind, you will be activating your senses and your emotions too, since all our memories are tagged with feeling. The knot in your stomach when Mary nearly causes a scandal by breaking social conventions? That knot is all yours. It is part of what connects you to the story.

This is what we mean by seeing the place as we read the text of a Gospel passage. Again we enter to see, hear, smell, and feel the scene. Here is one possible way we might imagine this text.

～

See a glistening leg of lamb being roasted over the fire and smell it as it comes from the clay oven, seasoned with garlic and rosemary and oregano. Maybe there is some herb-crusted veal or tenderloin too, with a nice balsamic reduction, since this is a party to celebrate that Lazarus is alive again. Martha cuts into the lamb; see the juices run onto the cutting board. Steam rises off a large dish of beans with slivered almonds as she brings it to the reclining guests. There is a bowl of warm olives with lemon zest and cardamom being passed around, and a board of freshly baked flatbread and hummus. There are figs and dates and goat cheese with honey on a platter in the center of the group. Everyone holds a cup brimming with the best red wine that Martha could find or beg from her neighbors. Imagine that you are there, enjoying the food and drink. Thaddeus and Andrew and James can't help smiling as they look across the room at Lazarus. They look at James and John and notice that they are smiling too. Jesus is at the center of it all, enjoying his friends. Everyone seems to be talking and laughing. See the joy on the faces lit up by the oil lamps that Martha has lit and placed around the room. This could have been a funeral wake for Lazarus. Instead, there is so much life here in the presence of Jesus that the room pulsates with it. Maybe you hear the sounds of music and dancing in the courtyard just beyond.

The dinner guests are stretched out on cushions, leaning on one elbow, free to reach for more flatbread and olives or lamb. Martha is moving around to make sure no one's cup is empty. But her eyes keep returning to Jesus. It is a real celebration, a banquet in Jesus' honor. Then something happens. Once again, as in Luke 10, Mary disrupts Martha's dinner party by breaking social conventions and doing something a little scandalous.

Here we might shift to try to watch Mary and see her actions. What would she have been feeling?

No one notices when, after clearing an empty platter, Mary slips away from the low table where all the food was laid out. Hidden away in one of the back rooms in a special chest, wrapped in fine linen, is her most precious possession. She hasn't stored up her small portion

of wealth in coins or jewels or anything else. But she has *this*. She has
a small stone jar, almost translucent, that holds about a pint of the
purest spikenard imported from northern India. The flask itself is
beautiful, and as she picks it up, cradling it in both hands, she can feel
the weight of it—in every sense. She can imagine the intensely fragrant
perfume, amber in color, sealed tightly in the delicate jar with its thin
neck. This is an heirloom, something to save for a solemn ceremonial
occasion of only the highest significance. But somehow she knows that
this is the time. The storm clouds are gathering around Jesus and his
enemies are plotting. She wants to give Jesus everything she has. If not
now, on this special night, then when?

With one swift movement she breaks the neck of the jar. Even
before she returns to the main room, the disciples and other guests can
smell this intense, earthy fragrance. See the heads turn. Peter and Nathaniel and Thomas are nearest, and they turn immediately to see
where the scent is coming from. It is musky and sweet at the same time,
but not cloying. All conversation stops mid-sentence as Mary comes
into the room, kneels by Jesus, and pours out the precious liquid on
his feet. She doesn't have a cloth, so she wipes his feet with her own
hair in an intimate gesture of purest love.

It is as if time is suspended; hardly anyone even breathes for a
minute. Light continues to pour in the window from the west. The
footfalls of a passerby can be heard on the cobblestones outside. And
that scent! Has anyone smelled this before? A few guests have a vivid
memory of the funeral of a beloved family member or friend. But
when they catch their breath again and realize what Mary has done,
they all have the same thought: a whole year's wages have been used
up in one act of extravagant love. They can hardly speak.

All of them, that is, except Judas. Clutching the leather moneybag,
where he kept the common purse for Jesus' disciples, jingling the
coins, he breaks the silence. Any remaining reverie is abruptly dissi-
pated as he voices his disgust at the sheer waste of Mary's gesture. See

the bitter expression on his face and hear the disdain in his voice when he says, "Why wasn't this perfume sold and the money given to the poor?" Feel the tension in the room. Notice the look on Mary's reddening face as he mocks her generous act of love and reduces it to a base financial transaction.

The room is still heavy with the fragrance of the perfume as Jesus defends Mary. See him stand up to face Judas. Hear his authority when he commands Judas: "Leave her alone. It was intended that she should save this perfume for the day of my burial." Perhaps he turns from facing Judas to look at all his friends and disciples around the table before adding: "You will always have the poor among you, but you will not always have me."

REFLECT

Now that we have entered vividly into the scene, let us hold it in our memory while we consider it from a few different angles.

Notice how gloriously this passage of Scripture begins in our English translation: "Jesus arrived at Bethany, where Lazarus *lived* . . ." (12:1). This could have been, should have been: "Jesus arrived at Bethany, where Lazarus *had died* . . ." But no—Bethany is where Lazarus *lived*! This plain and ordinary way of speaking, identifying the place where Jesus and the disciples go next, is suddenly charged with meaning. Grief is so deeply associated with particular places. How different this could have been! No wonder the narrator does not say, as in Luke 10, that they arrived at Martha's house. This is now the place where Lazarus lived. Let the reader understand.

Lazarus seems always to avoid the spotlight. He hadn't spoken when the sisters were fighting in Luke 10, nor even when he was raised from the dead in John 11. And now, here he is again, reclining at the table. But, of course, he is picked out and named among the guests, for the simple reason that he should be dead. He shouldn't be there.

Martha is the hostess again, working hard in the kitchen to prepare this meal, a meal given in Jesus' honor. We can imagine that this is an extraordinary banquet. After experiencing Jesus' life-giving grace, you throw a real party. Martha has obviously learned her lesson since Luke 10, and there is now no rebuke from Jesus. This time, she is not "distracted with much serving." The text says simply, "Martha served." Jesus is now the focus of attention, the one honored. Martha fully appreciates now that there is only one thing necessary.

Mary again disrupts Martha's dinner party with an unconventional and extravagant gesture. But this time, there is no sign of resentment from Martha.

In the Gospel of John, Jesus' first week of public ministry ends with a great feast at Cana. Now his final week begins with another feast. In both cases a certain extravagance is called forth. As Bruner has noted, there was an excess of wine on the one hand and an excess of perfume on the other. This was not a time for moderation.

In so much of life, we are called upon to exercise moderation: moderation in eating, moderation in drinking, moderation in spending, and so on. It is nice to think there is something about which you don't have to be moderate! What a relief. Is there somewhere you can be as extreme, excessive, and immoderate as you please? Yes! Here it is. At the feet of Jesus, you can pour out all your love, with nothing held back. All the tributaries of desire gather into this rushing cataract.

This is the last supper before the Last Supper. It's the next-to-last supper. Before that more famous meal with the disciples, Jesus eats this simple meal with his friends in Bethany. It is truly a table in the presence of his enemies (Psalm 23:5), for once Jesus had raised Lazarus, the opposition against him intensified. "From that day on," we read, "they plotted to take his life" (John 11:53). And immediately after this meal in Martha's house the events leading to his arrest and crucifixion are set in motion. In the midst of all this tension is a table like the one in Psalm 23 where there is an anointing and a cup that overflows.

Mary makes her offering to Jesus at the very moment he is being marked out for death by his enemies. This joyful act of extravagance and self-sacrifice called forth by the presence of Jesus is not, therefore, a matter of ostentatious self-display. Mary of Bethany directs our attention to Jesus. She invites us to identify with Jesus wholly without reserve, in life and in death, giving all of what we have, no matter the cost. As Ignatius of Antioch said on his way to martyrdom in the early second century, "Leave me to imitate the Passion of my God." Nothing held back.

In Luke's Gospel, Jesus reminds every disciple to "take up their cross daily" (Luke 9:23). To take up our cross is not only to endure great suffering, or to perform acts of great sacrifice, but to give all we have every moment of every ordinary day. Mary's consecration is something to be lived out every day, not just in a final act of martyrdom. In a short story, Flannery O'Connor narrates the thoughts of one of her young characters: "She could never be a saint, but she thought she could be a martyr if they killed her quick." Most of us can probably identify with that sentiment.

Meanwhile, we may still feast with Jesus "in the presence of our enemies." In a difficult season of our lives, we were loved by some amazing student friends from Texas who could afford to be generous. They knew something of what we were going through. One day one of them texted Bruce to say that he had discovered a restaurant app on his phone. Punching in the criteria of French cuisine, our neighborhood's location, and the highest possible price point (four dollar signs!), he found a restaurant. And so he and his wife took us out for what turned out to be one of the most exquisite meals of our lives. We will never forget that dinner. They wanted us to feel loved—and we did. We found laughter in the midst of tears. It was like sitting at a table with friends in the presence of our enemies.

And every week, Christians are invited to such a feast: the celebration of Holy Communion. At Holy Communion, we are invited to
look back and look forward. Looking back, we remember Christ's
death; looking ahead, we anticipate that we will eat with Christ anew
in paradise. And in the middle of our waiting, Christ comes and invites us to a table of joy, despite the darkness swirling around us. The
Lord's Supper is the epitome of a table in the wilderness. There is no
more glorious feast until the wedding supper of the Lamb (Revelation 19:9). Likewise, every meal, eaten in holiness, in its simple
goodness, reminds us of that banquet yet to come.

Let's go back to the scene at Bethany and consider it a little further.
In the midst of this festive meal, Jesus is anointed. As we have seen,
Mary breaks a flask and pours out a pint—about a half liter—of oil of
nard from India. The smell fills the room. In John 11, Martha was
worried about how Lazarus's corpse would smell if his tomb was disturbed. Here now is a sweet aroma, in contrast to the stench of death
that clung to Lazarus.

Mary seems to be known for being uninhibited and unconventional. She is acting in a rather shocking way by letting down her hair
among the men. Foot washing, if it was not done by slaves, was a
special sign of love; for Mary to wash Jesus' feet was the most intimate
of gestures. This is a reminder that love is not overcautious. The language of lovers always tends to hyperbole, and rightly so. Nobody
wants a marriage proposal that is drawn up as a contract of minimal
essential conditions.

We used to play a game with our daughter when she was young. It
might begin with one of us saying, "I love you more than chocolate."
Then the stakes would get raised, step by step. "Daddy, I love you more
than a million dollars." And then the reply, "I love you more than to
the moon and back." We knew it was getting really serious, though,
when she would say, "Mummy, I love you more than strawberries,"
since we knew how much she loved strawberries. That was just about

as much love as she could imagine. Love naturally tends to these heightened gestures.

Here, Mary of Bethany offers a gesture of love that shocks the other guests. As they would say when we lived in England, everyone was gobsmacked. If you glance back a chapter to the start of John 11, you'll see a clue to the significance of this anointing having made a big impression. John describes Lazarus as the brother of the Mary who did *this*, "the same one who poured perfume on the Lord and wiped his feet with her hair" (John 11:2). This is before the anointing itself is narrated in chapter 12. Literary critics would describe this as "proleptic": anticipating something that hasn't happened yet. "Yes," the narrator says, "we're talking about Lazarus, the brother of *that* Mary." She clearly had a reputation.

We might also reflect upon the wider context of anointing in Scripture. It is good to remember that "Christ" is not just a surname for Jesus. The word means "Messiah" or "the anointed one." The high priest Aaron was anointed in the Old Testament, as was the whole tabernacle and its furnishings (Exodus 30:30). Anointing was sacred. Israel's kings, beginning with Saul and David, were anointed (1 Samuel 10:1; 16:13). This sacred ritual was symbolic of the Holy Spirit, for after David was anointed, we read, "From that day on the Spirit of the LORD came powerfully upon David" (1 Samuel 16:13). Anointing was also, of course, associated with the rites of burial, as we find after Jesus' own death (Luke 23:56).

So what is Mary doing when she anoints Jesus' feet at this meal? Jesus is anointed by Mary as a sacred king and anointed as a burial ritual—anointed for a royal death, as Bruner observes. In John 11, Martha had understood that Jesus was the Christ, the Son of God. Here, Mary understands the costly, loving discipleship involved in following him. Bruner puts it so well: Martha honors the risen Lord; Mary, the dying Lord.

Mary's gift is estimated at about three hundred denarii, which our English translation helpfully explains was "worth a year's wages" (12:5). The buying power of one denarius is thought to have been the equivalent of roughly a day's wage for a common laborer, so that helps us get a sense of the costliness of Mary's gift.

Jesus called forth such generous and spontaneous love from his friends. Wouldn't you love to have been there? The scene at Bethany is one of pure joy and celebration in the presence of the One who is life itself. Joy, feasting, laughter, celebration, and friendship. Love and tears together. A night like this—you would want it never to end.

But in sharp contrast to Mary's anointing is Judas's act of fraud. You can't miss the parallelism. In complete contrast to the spontaneous generosity is the calculating betrayal. In complete contrast to the self-lessness of Mary is the selfishness of Judas. He made pretense of caring for the poor, but really, he was on the take.

We should pause to consider Judas's complaint about Mary's costly gift: "Why wasn't this perfume sold and the money given to the poor? It was worth a year's wages" (12:5).

There is, after all, a kind of worldly prudence in his proffered objection. When one commodity can be easily converted into another of the same value, we say it is "fungible." The most fungible thing of all is money: pure quantity with almost no qualities attached. Judas was doing the mental math. He wasn't just the keeper of the purse. He was a kind of accountant, thinking in terms of "effective altruism." He thought Mary's unique, unrepeatable, noninterchangeable act of love could be reduced to a financial transaction like any other. What is the credit to enter for this debit?

But of course, even this kind of objection requires a framework of value, and the one that Judas was putting forward was sheer pretense. It was a plausible abstraction, an affectation of charitable concern. One of the clues to this is the abstract phrase "the poor."

Enormous violence has been done in recent centuries on behalf of abstract groups like "the poor." One thinks of the millions sent to the gulags in the Soviet Union to serve an ideology ostensibly devoted to the poor. We might take it as a general rule that any ideology that neglects the poor right in front of us, or that loses sight of the person of Jesus, will fail us. Jesus is the greatest lover of the poor. Indeed, he so strongly identifies with the poor that he says, "Whatever you did for one of the least of these brothers and sisters of mine, you did for me" (Matthew 25:40; see also Matthew 10:42). And at this moment in John's Gospel, Jesus is the poorest man in Bethany, and Mary is sacrificially serving him.

Historically, it is precisely such devoted, self-sacrificial disciples who have been most faithful in relief and development work, ministering in inner cities, caring for those with communicable diseases, and giving of themselves in other situations of unrelieved suffering. It takes a great love to make a great sacrifice.

The Hawaiian island of Molokai is not a spot on the usual tourist itinerary. It is a place that has seen much suffering and economic hardship, past and present. The island slopes from high mountainous rainforest in the east to arid grasslands and sandy beaches in the west. But in about the middle of the island, on the north side, there is a caldera—a kind of crater from a sunken volcano. A sheer cliff face of two thousand feet separates it from the rest of the island, and the path down is so steep that the caldera can only be easily reached by sea. The small peninsula is called Kalaupapa; today, it is a national park. It preserves the memories of great suffering and great love, for during the nineteenth century, it was the site of a leper colony. We once rode mules down the switchback trails from the top side to visit the caldera, for we knew the story of a man called Father Damien, and we wanted to see his place of ministry for ourselves.

Once leprosy (now known as Hansen's disease) was introduced to the islands, Hawaiians were particularly susceptible to the illness. During the nineteenth century, any Hawaiians infected were declared legally dead and sent by ship to be quarantined permanently at Kalaupapa. If they were unwilling to disembark, they were tossed overboard into the sea. Father Damien was a Belgian priest who volunteered to go and minister among the six hundred lepers there. He wanted to create a community of love where there was none. For sixteen years he dressed wounds, built homes and furniture, made coffins, and dug graves. He created a community and built a church. Eventually, he contracted leprosy and died of the disease.

He had given everything he had. As we walked among the ruins of the houses he had built and sat in his church, we kept thinking of him. This was a place of so much sadness and so much love. Like Mary of Bethany, Father Damien held nothing back. This kind of selflessness demonstrates profound love for Jesus: when we give to others, we give to Jesus, and when we give to Jesus, we give to others.

As we return to the scene in Bethany, we might notice that Jesus defends Mary as he had earlier. To Judas he says, "Leave her alone." Previously, Jesus defended her against her sister's resentment. Now he defends her against Judas's condemnation. Once more, Mary has chosen the better part. First she sat at Jesus' feet in faith; then she fell at his feet in hope; now she anoints his feet in love. Jesus was the supreme object of all her love. Taking your place with Mary of Bethany at the feet of Jesus may well incur the disapproval of others—as Mary found over and over. But isn't it good to know that Jesus will defend you too as you take risks in loving adoration and service of him? Even when others don't understand, he sees and receives the love offered to him from a pure heart.

By the end of this Scripture passage, we realize that Jesus has been anointed for burial ahead of time. The stage is set for his exaltation through suffering unto death. It all commences now. At least four times earlier in this Gospel, Jesus (or the Gospel narrator) has said that his "time" or his "hour" has not yet come. But now the hour has come. In John's Gospel, suffering and death are the path to Jesus' glory; here, the "book of glory" begins. Indeed, just a few verses after the banquet, Jesus will say, "The hour has come for the Son of Man to be glorified" (12:23). The curtain has been raised, and the climactic act has begun.

We take our place again with Mary, and we watch Jesus go on to do what he alone can do. We are his followers and his friends. We choose to follow this path of cruciform discipleship, love, and sacrifice.

What is your pint of nard?

RESPOND

Having prepared ourselves, having made an effort to enter the scene of this Scripture with our senses, and having pondered the words and actions, we are ready to enter into conversation with God and pray out of this Scripture.

Take a few moments to return to the text itself (John 12:1-8) and read through the passage slowly one more time. Ask yourself again what you see, hear, smell, and feel. Watch the individuals at the center of the action and hear the dialogue as if you were there in the house. Place yourself back in the scene in your imagination, as if you are really there around the table witnessing every word and action. Imagine that you are one of the characters; see with their eyes and hear with their ears. Place yourself particularly with Mary of Bethany, in prostrate adoration at the feet of Jesus. Substitute yourself into her place in the scene.

You may already have begun to notice certain things from the words of this passage. What words arrested you or seemed as if they were underlined? A number of painters, especially in the seventeenth century, used dramatic lighting to spotlight certain elements in a scene, directing our gaze to one or more of the subjects. Maybe something like that has happened already for you. If it has, it is worth paying attention to this as an invitation to return and pray more here.

As previously, we offer some questions below to help prompt your own conversation with God out of this Scripture. But we should emphasize once more that you need not approach these questions like a homework assignment to complete from beginning to end. It may be, in the freedom of God's Spirit, that just one of these questions is important for you today. Perhaps you can leave the rest for some later time. In your own very personal conversation with Christ, the questions themselves can fall away like scaffolding.

- When you have experienced Jesus as the resurrection—when you have trusted him and seen the glory of God—then everything else is revalued in the light of your desire to adore him. Notice the transition after Lazarus's resurrection from grief to joy: a dinner in Jesus' honor and Mary's costly gift. Take time to express your gratitude to God as you ponder similar experiences of his grace in your own life. What would you like to say to him as you see him revealed in this Scripture?

- Have you given anything in the past to God that others judged to be wasteful? Picture Jesus receiving your gift, defending you from accusation. How does this change your memory of that experience?

- Notice Mary's reckless disregard, her absence of prudence, in matters of both social and financial propriety. Are there ways that worldly prudence holds you back from a more radical and entire adoration of Jesus? How would you express your love for Jesus if you didn't care about what people think?

- Mary arrived at a place where she was ready to give up everything in service of Jesus Christ. Perhaps you are in the midst of a big decision in your own life. Could this be an opportunity for deeper dedication to Jesus? What might Jesus be asking of you? What do you want to say to him or do for him?

- The pint of nard for anointing was costly, worth a year's wages. What is your pint of nard today? What would it mean to pour it out on the feet of Jesus? As you take your place alongside Mary of Bethany, is there anything you feel called by God to do with your time or money?

- Notice the contrast between Mary's sacrificial consecration and Judas's calculating betrayal. One keeps nothing in reserve; the other steals a little for himself. Is there anywhere in your life where you sense God calling you away from betrayal—even small pilfering—toward a love that holds nothing back? Hold this passage up like a mirror. Can you identify an area of your life where the Spirit is convicting you?

- Jesus defends Mary's extravagance even in the face of pressing needs, such as the plight of the poor. Every other good becomes a relative good in the presence of Jesus. What are the pressing needs around you (even those that are truly legitimate) that might distract you from making the adoration of Jesus the primary thing in your life? What is the still, small voice of the Lord saying to you about expectations you must ignore and release in order to serve him—*including* expectations concerning the urgent needs of others?

REVIEW

Before concluding this time of prayer, review any notes you have made and look back to see if anything particular seemed highlighted for you as you prayed. What was the place of your most significant encounter with Jesus in this passage? Stay to savor the experience. After a fine meal on a special occasion, you wouldn't just rush away after the last bite. Take a few moments to write down any insights, decisions, or new directions prompted by your meditation on Jesus' last meal in the home of Mary and Martha and Lazarus. Notice in particular if there is something you feel called by God to do.

We prayed earlier, "Lord, deepen my love." It might be fitting now to pray the last verse of Frances Havergal's hymn "Take My Life and Let It Be":

Take my love; my Lord, I pour
at thy feet its treasure store.
Take myself, and I will be
ever, only, all for thee,
ever, only, all for thee.

When you are ready, blowing out your candle one last time, you might want to conclude this session by gathering it all up and offering it to God in the words of a fitting prayer such as the Lord's Prayer or the doxology.

5

AT THE FEET OF JESUS

Looking Back on the Retreat

HAVE YOU EVER BEEN ASKED, "How are you?" only to realize that you have no idea of the answer? So often we just plunge on in the stream of activity, one thing after another, without pausing for reflection. It can be hard to find time to ask ourselves, "I wonder what God was saying to me there," or "I wonder if my heart was resistant there to something God was doing."

For many centuries, Protestants and Catholics alike have thought it important to take time in prayer to review what has been going on in our lives and our communities. We might look back with God at the day, or the week, or a longer season of our lives. In the seventeenth century, it was common for Puritans and Jesuits to call this a prayer of *examination*.

Hopefully this does not conjure up images of an examination at school, with rows of desks and a list of questions that you might get wrong—or, even worse, an invasive examination in a doctor's office with metal instruments, antiseptic smells, bright lights, and white lab coats. If so, we need to find another word, and fast. Think of this as a prayerful review. Some people call it "praying backwards," since you are casting your mind back to remember and to talk with God about what he has been doing in your life.

As you reach the end of this little book, it is worth looking back over our sessions in Scripture to harvest the good fruits of the Holy Spirit's work in us. We can do a prayerful review at the feet of Jesus.

As we have followed Mary of Bethany, we have seen her movement of deeper and deeper prostration: from sitting at the feet of Jesus in faith, to falling at the feet of Jesus in hope, to anointing the feet of Jesus in love. Ask for God's help to follow this movement in your own affections. Let's pause over this for a little, praying over each movement.

SITTING AT JESUS' FEET IN FAITH

Take a moment to look back over the first meditation on Luke 10, when Jesus first came to Martha's house. Martha was busy, distracted, and troubled with many things, but Mary was content to sit at Jesus' feet and listen to his teaching. She was commended for choosing the one thing necessary.

As you review your own work, seeing and reflecting and praying out of this passage, are there one or two things that stand out? How have you encountered Jesus Christ? How will you live differently as a result? What do you want to remember a month from now, a year from now, or for the rest of your life? Take some time to write this down in a journal or save a note somewhere you can return to later. Does anyone come to mind who could listen to what you have discovered in prayer? Perhaps you could set up a time to talk. You might want to write a note to them later today, or even right now. All this might help to fix these insights in place so they don't get lost in the press of the many things that keep coming at us, like water from a never-ending fire hose.

FALLING AT JESUS' FEET IN HOPE

Our second passage of Scripture was the longest and most dramatic. In John 11, Jesus delayed coming to the aid of his friends even after hearing that Lazarus was sick and in critical condition. He arrived (seemingly) too late and had three intimate meetings outside the home: one with Martha, one with Mary, and one climactic meeting with Lazarus. In the middle of this passage, we noticed that Mary was again at the feet of Jesus, but this time she was laid out flat in grief and unrelieved sorrow. She fell at the feet of Jesus, her last and only hope.

Take time now to review your meditation on this passage in company with God. This is not so much to do all the work over again as it is to look back over your own experience of these things. Again, what stood out to you? Is there anything more the Spirit of God is highlighting for you? Open your heart to the surprise that there is something *more* for you to receive, even now.

Jesus is the same yesterday, today, and forever, and he continues to speak to us today through his word. The Anglican poet John Donne once coined the beautiful image that in God's economy it is always autumn: "In paradise, the fruits were ripe, the first minute, and in heaven it is always Autumn, his mercies are ever in their maturity." We ask for our daily bread, and God never says, "Oh, too bad! You should have come yesterday." And he never says, "Oh, too bad! You must come instead tomorrow." No, "*Today, if you will hear his voice*, today, he will hear you."

The harvest is always ripe in the kingdom of God. So, as you walk through your notes and your memory of praying over this passage, what can you harvest? What seems most important for you? What is God saying *today*? What is he asking of you? There will be something uniquely and irreplaceably for you. What is it?

Again, write this down, tell a friend about it, and lodge these insights in your own heart where they will be long remembered.

ANOINTING AT JESUS' FEET IN LOVE

Finally, we returned to the home of Martha, Mary, and Lazarus for a celebratory meal, the second-to-last supper. We observed not only a rich feast among friends and followers of Jesus, but we saw the joy on the face of each one, for Jesus had done the impossible by returning Lazarus to them alive and well. Instead of a wake, this was a party full to the brim with life. We followed Mary of Bethany again, like there was a spotlight tracking her. We saw her pour out her costly gift, and with it all her love, anointing the feet of Jesus. As he himself recognized, she did this in anticipation of his burial.

In sharp contrast, we watched the calculating betrayal of Judas as he pretended to a kind of moral outrage at Mary's wastefulness. This perfume could have been sold, and the money better given to the poor. In truth, he was interested in turning this treasure into coins only because he was secretly embezzling from the common fund. All this was an indication for us that this amazing meal was in fact a table in the presence of Jesus' enemies. The storm clouds were gathering, and Jesus was headed toward the cross.

What was your experience like in this third session as you meditated on the narrative of the anointing (and the betrayal)? Think back over preparing in prayer, seeing the place, reflecting upon it all, and finally conversing with God more personally out of the passage. Viewing it all more simply now, rather than in detail, what stands out? How are you being called to pour out your love at the feet of Jesus? What remains and seems especially significant for you? Is there something you would like to linger over a little longer in prayer?

When you're ready, you can write or talk with a friend, or otherwise fix these insights as something that will stay with you. Francis de Sales likened meditation to taking a walk in a walled garden. The very last step, he said, was like taking one flower and pinning it to your lapel to take with you as you leave. As you shut the door, leave the garden, and return to daily life, the flower is still pinned to your coat as a reminder of those things that were precious to you and that you do not want to forget.

FAITH, HOPE, AND LOVE

We mentioned earlier that for most of Christian history, theologians thought of our souls as constituted by memory, reason, and will. In fact, each of our meditations followed this pattern of using these faculties ("all our powers") to engage Scripture together. When John of the Cross came to consider our capacity to reach God and genuinely encounter him, he realized that there was a fundamental problem. Our powers were not up to the task. God is infinite and we are finite. And as if that were not problem enough: God is holy and we are sinful.

So, what are we to do? John of the Cross recognized that we need the help of the Holy Spirit. We need these theological virtues to be "supernaturally infused" in us. As we try to reach God with our intellect, our understanding can only go so far. In the end, it is just not equal to the task. We need to experience a kind of vertigo in the presence of God—as if we are lost in the dark—if it is truly God whom we are encountering. This ought rightly to be a kind of shattering experience. Our minds cannot contain him. Our minds are too corrupted and soiled with sin. It is the work of the Holy Spirit, in the intimacy of darkness, as it were, to work faith in the soul. It is the gift of God as, like Mary, we sit at Jesus' feet and receive his teaching in our hearts. Here we sit, and our faith deepens as we realize more and more who Jesus is.

Perhaps even more poignantly, John of the Cross realized that our memory (and imagination) is not capable of God without the supernatural work of the Spirit. The older we get, the more regrets we inevitably have—if we have been paying attention at all. We accumulate scars and injuries both from things done to us and the things that we have done. By the grace of God, there is much stored up in our memories, much to furnish our imaginations, that is very good. But oh, how deeply we need the Holy Spirit to infuse hope in our memories and to inspire hope in our imaginations for the future. Our frail and flawed

memories need, in a sense, to go dark to allow the light of something
more to enter—the light of the resurrection itself. With Mary, we fall
at Jesus' feet in hope. He is the resurrection and the life. We can say to
ourselves: *I am not going anywhere else, but I will allow my hope to grow
brighter and brighter and brighter right here, until he makes all
things new.*

And now, like waiting for the third note in a chord, we move from
faith and hope to love. John of the Cross knew that our wills could
not—not with all our best efforts and earnestness—attain to God's will.
There will always be something that falls short. Once more, any focus
on our own anxious efforts must somehow be dimmed and over-
shadowed by the surpassing, unique work of the Holy Spirit. God by
his Spirit can join himself to our wills and strengthen us to love him
as he ought to be loved: as our highest, best, supreme desire. With
Mary of Bethany, we hold nothing back and we anoint Jesus' feet
in love.

In the end, the insight here is that to be really human—to be what
we were meant to be—we need to be filled with the Holy Spirit. We
long to be conformed to the image of Christ and for his character to
be imprinted on us (Romans 8:29). For this we need to be filled, sealed,
anointed, and indwelt by the Spirit of Jesus. In this is the fulfillment of
our human nature. We are meant to experience the presence of God.
The presence of God that was the perfecting element of human nature
was lost in the garden of Eden when humans sinned and rebelled
against their Creator. By the work of Christ and the gift of the Holy
Spirit, that presence of God in human persons is restored.

So, it is by God's grace and mercy that we are enabled to stand upright in the presence of love itself, raised to the dignity of a human
person as God intended.

With Mary of Bethany, we begin at the feet of Jesus, and there we
learn of faith, hope, and love. Faith in Jesus Christ. Hope in Jesus
Christ. Love for Jesus Christ. But like the bent and crippled woman

whom Jesus encounters in Luke 13, we are healed in his presence and made to stand upright in his company, restored to dignity. "When Jesus saw her, he called her forward and said to her, 'Woman, you are set free from your infirmity.' Then he put his hands on her, and immediately she straightened up and praised God" (Luke 13:12-13). As she straightened up, shoulders back, and looked ahead, she gazed into the beautiful face of Jesus.

You were made for this, and so are we. This is where we are headed. We take our place in humility now at Jesus' feet, but we look forward to the day we will all see Jesus face to face. As the apostle Paul wrote, "For now we see only a reflection as in a mirror; then we shall see face to face. Now I know in part; then I shall know fully, even as I am fully known. And now these three remain: faith, hope and love. But the greatest of these is love" (1 Corinthians 13:12-13).

6

A NOTE ON MARY OF BETHANY, MARY MAGDALENE, AND THE SINFUL WOMAN

LUKE'S GOSPEL IDENTIFIES MARY as the sister of Martha. From the Gospel of John, we also learn that she and Martha were the sisters of Lazarus, and that the three siblings lived in the village of Bethany. John also narrates Mary's costly anointing of Jesus' feet, wiping his feet with her hair.

There are other accounts of the anointing of Jesus, and this has caused some confusion for readers past and present. It probably adds to the confusion that so many women in the Gospels are named Mary!

Matthew and Mark include stories of the anointing of Jesus' head by an unnamed woman (Matthew 26:6; Mark 14:1). Luke includes a similar account in which Jesus, dining at the house of Simon the Pharisee, has his feet anointed by a sinful woman whom he had forgiven. Just a few verses later, Luke introduces Mary Magdalene "from whom seven demons had come out," but without any suggestion that she was the sinful woman just previously described (Luke 7:36-50; 8:2).

Nevertheless, some of the early church fathers, such as Augustine and Gregory the Great, conflated Mary of Bethany, the sinful woman, and Mary Magdalene all together. These three figures merged into one.

Centuries later, the story of yet another Mary, the penitent hermit Mary of Egypt (from about the fifth century), was mixed in as well. *The Penitent Magdalene*, a poignant sculpture by Donatello from the mid-fifteenth century, is on display at the Duomo Museum in Florence. It perfectly witnesses to the fusion of all these elements in a moving work of religious devotion. Worn and aged, Mary reaches out with hands just coming together in prayer. She knows she is in need of mercy and is also confident of receiving it. In one exhibition, the sculpture was placed opposite a sculpture of a crucifixion. Mary was looking in prayer to Jesus to the very end of her life.

For these earlier writers and artists, their first concern was not necessarily to do the sort of historical criticism that would distinguish separate biographies for these women—the sort of critical scholarship that one can find in the careful account given in the *Anchor Bible Dictionary* of the women named Mary in the New Testament.

No, the primary concern of these church fathers (as for Christian artists) was to follow the edifying and pastorally significant themes that emerged as they contemplated these accounts. It is no surprise that they found overlapping and mutually illuminating themes: contrition, forgiveness, self-offering, and love. The spiritual continuities were more important to them than the historical discontinuities, especially since these spiritual elements were so potent and real. These spiritual continuities also built a bridge from these accounts into the present.

Consider the phenomenon of telescoping or foreshortening when viewing nearer objects against a more distant background. We visited the Leaning Tower of Pisa some years ago, and we walked around the vast lawn that surrounds the tower and the cathedral. It was filled with tourists having fun taking pictures, composing shots that created the visual illusion of people in the foreground holding the leaning tower between their fingers.

One could hold up one's thumb and forefinger, spread apart, and then the person with the camera only had to move around and zoom in or out, until the distant image of the tower fit right between the fingers. Presto, you had a photograph of someone holding a miniature leaning tower of Pisa. (Okay, we confess, we took a few of those pictures too.)

This example of foreshortening is silly, but it might still help us think about someone seeing distinct and separate objects in one plane of vision.

Perhaps we should imagine an interpreter like Augustine doing a sort of telescoping, taking a long view of Mary Magdalene (a major figure in all the gospels, present at the crucifixion, burial, and resurrection), but then seeing just a little further on, over her shoulder, the "sinful woman," and then a bit further on yet, the image of Mary of Bethany. These were all women who loved Jesus. Foreshortened, these three images would shift and then merge together, especially if you were adjusting your lens to contemplate specifically how these stories might help you to respond personally to Jesus for yourself.

We are doing something different in this retreat. We have focused specifically on the three passages where we encounter Mary of Bethany without drawing in these other stories. But like Augustine, you may find yourself wondering about these other accounts. You may want to ponder further the anointing stories in Matthew 26:6-13; Mark 14:3-19; and Luke 7:36-50. To follow Mary Magdalene, you can find her introduced in Luke 8:2, and then trace her response to Jesus in each of the Gospel accounts of the cross and the empty tomb. There is a good review of these passages in Craig Keener's commentary on John.

In each of these episodes we have another opportunity to place ourselves in the narrative alongside those who encountered Jesus. With them we respond in repentance, wonder, love, and adoration. With them we draw near to the Christ who is the same yesterday, today, and forever.

NOTES

INTRODUCTION

8   *The face of God for now:* Augustine, commenting on Psalm 68, in *Sermons II (20-50) on the Old Testament*, The Works of St. Augustine: A Translation for the 21st Century, trans. Edmund Hill (Brooklyn: New City, 1990), 46, sermon 22.7.

     The one eternal Word: See Hans Urs von Balthasar, *Prayer* (San Francisco: Ignatius, 1986), 18.

     Full volume of the divine voice: Balthasar, *Prayer*, 19.

9   *He can never be simply past tense:* See Balthasar, *Prayer*, 14.

11   *Modern psychologists and therapists:* See, e.g., T. M. Luhrmann, *When God Talks Back: Understanding the American Evangelical Relationship with God* (New York: Knopf, 2012), 72-100.

12   *"Lives" of Christ:* The most important was from Ludolf of Saxony, *The Life of Jesus Christ*, trans. Milton T. Walsh, 4 vols., Cistercian Studies Series 267 (Collegeville, MN: Cistercian Publications, 2018).

     "Composition" or "seeing the place": Ignatius of Loyola, *Personal Writings*, Penguin Classics (London: Penguin, 1996), 294.

     Puritans encouraged a similar practice: See, e.g., the fourth part of Richard Baxter, *The Saint's Everlasting Rest* (Vancouver: Regent College Publishing, 2004), which has the splendid description in the original subtitle, "Containing a Directory for the getting and keeping of the Heart in Heaven: By the diligent practice of that Excellent unknown Duty of Heavenly Meditation. Being the main thing intended by the Author, in the writing of this Book; and to which all the rest is but subservient."

13   *Accounts of first-century Palestine:* See especially Craig S. Keener, *The IVP Bible Background Commentary: New Testament*, 2nd ed. (Downers Grove,

IL: InterVarsity Press, 2014). See also Keener's online resources at https://craigkeener.com/about-craig/.

14 *Love desires to have the beloved*: Balthasar, *Prayer*, 129.

15 *O my heart, my heart*: Francis de Sales, *Introduction to the Devout Life*, trans. John K. Ryan (New York: Image Books, 1972), 74.

O most merciful Redeemer: See further David Farmer, ed., "Richard of Chichester," in *The Oxford Dictionary of Saints* (Oxford: Oxford University Press, 2011).

16 *All our powers*: Ignatius writes of using our "three powers" (memory, understanding, and will) in prayer in the *Spiritual Exercises*. See, e.g., Ignatius of Loyola, *Personal Writings*, 294-96.

We've provided a historical note: See further: Ignatius, *Personal Writings*; Francis de Sales, *Introduction to the Devout Life*, trans. John K. Ryan (New York: Image Books, 1972); Richard Baxter, *The Saint's Everlasting Rest* (Vancouver: Regent College Publishing, 2004), part IV.

Prepare our hearts: These steps are adapted from Timothy M. Gallagher, *Meditation and Contemplation: An Ignatian Guide to Praying with Scripture* (New York: Crossroad, 2008).

17 *Ignatius of Loyola used to take*: Ignatius, *Personal Writings*, 300.

"A leap of the child": Hans Urs von Balthasar, *Christian Meditation* (San Francisco: Ignatius, 1984), 20.

20 *This is where our meditation proper begins*: In the *Spiritual Exercises*, Ignatius would distinguish between contemplation of visible episodes in Scripture, where you use your memory and imagination, and meditation on didactic passages of teaching, where you focus more on the words. Here we combine both modes of prayerful engagement, as we both "see" the Gospel story and then also "reflect" on it.

Moving through the passage: Gallagher, *Meditation and Contemplation*, 17; Ignatius, *Personal Writings*, 306-8.

22 *In each of the sessions*: This is similar to what is sometimes called in an Ignatian context a preached retreat or guided meditation.

The desert father John Cassian: John Cassian, *Conferences*, trans. Colin Luibheid (New York: Paulist Press, 1985), 58.

The Puritan Richard Baxter: Baxter, *Saint's Everlasting Rest*, 138-39.

23 *Francis de Sales thought*: Francis de Sales, *Introduction*, 80.

2. FIRST MEDITATION

33   One "who is visible": Ignatius of Loyola, *Personal Writings,* Penguin Classics (London: Penguin, 1996), 294.

37   *Rabbis generally did not include women*: R. Kent Hughes, *Luke, Volume One: That You May Know the Truth* (Wheaton, IL: Crossway, 1998), 396.

40   *A reservoir rather than a conduit*: Bernard of Clairvaux, *On the Song of Songs I* (Collegeville, MN: Cistercian Publications, 1971), 134.

41   *Liquid modernity*: Zygmunt Bauman, *Liquid Modernity* (Cambridge, UK: Blackwell, 2000).

42   *As Dante wrote:* Dante Alighieri, *Paradiso*, trans. Robert Hollander and Jean Hollander (New York: Anchor Books, 2007), 917 (Canto xxxiii.145).

43   *Teresa of Avila told her sisters:* Teresa of Avila, *The Interior Castle*, Classics of Western Spirituality (New York: Paulist Press, 1979), 192.
     First and second things: C. S. Lewis, *God in the Dock and Other Essays*, ed. Walter Hooper (Grand Rapids, MI: Eerdmans, 1970), 278-81.

45   *A kind of martial art*: David Allen, *Getting Things Done: The Art of Stress-Free Productivity*, rev. ed. (New York: Penguin Books, 2015), 11.

48   *Martha by Heather Kaufmann:* Heather Kaufmann, "Martha," *Ekstasis*, accessed October 15, 2024, www.ekstasismagazine.com/poetry/2022/martha. Used with permission of the author.

51   *My soul is like a house*: Augustine, *Confessions*, trans. R. S. Pine-Coffin, Penguin Classics (New York: Dorset Press, 1961), 24.

3. SECOND MEDITATION

56   *An old tradition, and a strong modern scholarly opinion*: The tradition goes back at least to the Latin church father Jerome. See Brian J. Caper, "Essene Community Houses and Jesus' Early Community," in James H. Charlesworth, ed., *Jesus and Archaeology* (Grand Rapids, MI: Eerdmans, 2006), 474-502, especially the discussion on 497-98. See also Gerald L. Borchert, *John 1-11: An Exegetical and Theological Exposition of Holy Scripture*, (Nashville: Broadman and Holman, 1996), 349.

57   *Frederick Dale Bruner's commentary:* Frederick Dale Bruner, *The Gospel of John: A Commentary* (Grand Rapids, MI: Eerdmans, 2012), 664-86.

61   *The highest statement yet:* Craig S. Keener, *The Gospel of John: A Commentary* (Peabody, MA: Hendrickson Publishers, 2003), 2:844-45.
     Equivalent of Peter's confession: R. Kent Hughes, *Luke, Volume One: That You May Know the Truth* (Wheaton, IL: Crossway, 1998), 399-400.

62   *A mini-resurrection within the story:* Bruner, *Gospel of John*, 674-75.

62   *As Frederick Dale Bruner says:* Bruner, *Gospel of John*, 675.

64   *Horses that are snorting and chafing:* There is a careful discussion of the
      Greek vocabulary in these verses in Andreas J. Köstenberger, *John*, Baker
      Exegetical Commentary on the New Testament (Grand Rapids, MI: Baker
      Academic, 2004), 339-40.

65   *The meeting with Lazarus:* See this short video by biblical scholar Craig
      Keener from the traditional site of Lazarus's tomb at Al-Eizariya: https://
      craigkeener.com/lazaruss-tomb/.

67   *A poignant poem reflecting on Lazarus's experience:* "Stephen to Lazarus,"
      C. S. Lewis, *Poems* (London: Geoffrey Bles, 1964), 125.
      The Heidelberg catechism: This catechism can be accessed at www.crcna.org
      /welcome/beliefs/confessions/heidelberg-catechism.

69   *Let us hear and rise again:* Augustine, "Tractate 49 on the Gospel of John,"
      in Philip Schaff, ed., *Nicene and Post-Nicene Fathers*: First Series (Peabody,
      MA: Hendrickson Publishers, 1994), 7:270-78.

4. THIRD MEDITATION

74   *Come Holy Spirit, fill the hearts:* Church of England and Society of
      St. Francis, eds., *Celebrating Common Prayer: A Version of the Daily Office,
      SSF* (London: Mowbray, 1992), 43.

78   *As Bruner has noted:* Frederick Dale Bruner, *The Gospel of John: A Com-
      mentary* (Grand Rapids, MI: Eerdmans, 2012), 702.

79   *As Ignatius of Antioch said:* Ignatius of Antioch, "Epistle to the Romans," in
      Maxwell Staniforth, ed., *Early Christian Writings: The Apostolic Fathers*
      (London: Penguin, 1987), 87.
      She could never be a saint: Flannery O'Connor, "A Temple of the Holy
      Ghost," in *A Good Man is Hard to Find and Other Short Stories* (New York:
      Harcourt Brace Jovanovich, 1976), 94.

81   *Martha honors the risen Lord*: Bruner, *Gospel of John*, 702.

84   *Father Damien was a Belgian priest:* Jan de Volder, *The Spirit of Father
      Damien: The Leper Priest—A Saint for Our Times*, trans. John Allen (San
      Francisco: Ignatius, 2010).

88   *Take my life and let it be:* Frances Havergal, "Take My Life and Let It Be,"
      1874, accessed October 16, 2024, https://hymnary.org/text/take_my_life
      _and_let_it_be.

5. AT THE FEET OF JESUS

89   *Prayer of examination:* Among the Puritans, see, e.g., Richard Rogers, *Seven
      Treatises* (n.p.: London, 1603): "It is a looking back, calling to mind, and

going through (so near as possibly we can) all the several actions of the day past, from the time of our first awaking out of sleep, to the time of our lying down to sleep again; to see how far forth we have walked with God, and wherein we have wandered from him: that we may be comforted in our well doing, humbled for our sins, and made more cheerful to do good, and more careful to avoid evil" (468). In Ignatius of Loyola, see *Personal Writings*, Penguin Classics (London: Penguin, 1996), 291-93. See also the modern adaptation in Timothy M. Gallagher, *The Examen Prayer: Ignatian Wisdom for Our Lives Today* (New York: Crossroad, 2006).

91   *In paradise, the fruits were ripe:* Evelyn M. Simpson, ed., *John Donne's Sermons on the Psalms and Gospels* (Berkeley, CA: University of California Press, 1963), 182.

92   *Francis de Sales likened meditation:* Francis de Sales, *Introduction to the Devout Life* (New York: Image Books, 1972), 79.

93   *John of the Cross came to consider:* Kieran Kavanaugh, ed., *John of the Cross: Selected Writings*, The Classics of Western Spirituality (New York: Paulist Press, 1987), 198-209.

6. A NOTE ON MARY OF BETHANY, MARY MAGDALENE, AND THE SINFUL WOMAN

98   *The women named Mary:* Raymond F. Collins, "Mary," in David Noel Freedman, ed., *The Anchor Bible Dictionary* (New York: Doubleday, 1992), 4:579-81.

99   *Craig Keener's commentary on John:* Craig Keener, *The Gospel of John: A Commentary* (Peabody, MA: Hendrickson, 2003), 2:859-61.